Coming Back to the Kingdom of God

Die to Sin and Renew Our Minds to God
John 3:5
Reconciling Our Desire and God's Reason

Bill Mitchell

WESTBOW
P R E S S®
A DIVISION OF THOMAS NELSON
& ZONDERVAN

WestBow Press books may be ordered through booksellers or by contacting:

WestBow Press
A Division of Thomas Nelson & Zondervan
1663 Liberty Drive
Bloomington, IN 47403
www.westbowpress.com
1 (866) 928-1240

ISBN: 978-1-9736-9587-5 (sc)
ISBN: 978-1-9736-9586-8 (hc)
ISBN: 978-1-9736-9588-2 (e)

Library of Congress Control Number: 2020912883

Print information available on the last page.

WestBow Press rev. date: 08/28/2020

Dedicated to everyone.

Most assuredly, I say to you, unless one is born of water
and the Spirit, he cannot enter the kingdom of God.
—John 3:5

Contents

Preface

OF ALL THE things I have worked for in my life, none is more important than my understanding of what God has given to us. God gave us a Kingdom; we just need to take it. My name is Bill Mitchell and I have been a member of the Lord's body for over twenty-five years. I have been a part of what our Lord died to give us the opportunity to have.

I am married and have three children who are grown and now taking on the monumental task of living life as God has asked us to live amongst a world that only wishes to divide us. Unlike my wife and I, our children grew up knowing God. (I can assure you this is not a guarantee they will understand and renew their minds as God desires). Life has become that we who desire to live faithfully sow our children among thorns. For now, there is no end in sight to this tangled chaos. For those who do not know God, this is not a problem for them now. Most believe life is just fine as it is. But I tell you these do not know any different. It is. "The cares of this world, the deceitfulness of riches, and the desires for other things entering in choke the word, and it becomes unfruitful" (see Mark 4:18 – 19). Rare is it that adults and children will remain faithful bearing good fruit even as they are sown on the good ground (see Mark 4:20). But what of the child who does not even know God exists? What then? Is there any hope at all for them? Yes, but only if they look to God.

I did not grow up knowing God. Instead, I grew up outside of what God has prepared for all people to know. Growing up in this manner kept me from the understanding of how a God fearing father disciplines in love. I needed this understanding as my wife and I raised our family. Because I was training myself as we were raising our children, we have had to endure what a lack of godly behavior brings to the innocent. This lack of godly behavior, if unchecked, is what emboldens generations of people to act out against what our Lord has purposed in Himself, and that is to bring us to God. So it is our convictions we must learn to change according to the knowledge of God. For us to be right in the sight of God, we must be willing to turn back to God. This is why we have God's Word.

What I have written, I have written for the purpose of telling all who read this book that we have been given instructions to get back to God. This is for all people. God gave two conditions for all: repent and die to sin. This means a person needs to live as God has instructed and become sinless. But how do we become sinless? As the Jews were the chosen of God, to live according to His purpose, we all now have the ability to come back to God for the purpose of our salvation. Jesus Christ has given us this way. This is to all who will obey.

In Luke 24, after the crucifixion of our Lord, He was raised from the dead and walked among the disciples. The disciples did not recognize Him. He asked,

> "What kind of conversation is this that you have with one another as you walk and are sad?" Cleopas answered, "Are you the only stranger in Jerusalem and have you not known the things which happened there in these days?" Jesus said, "What things?"

And the disciples said,

"The things concerning Jesus of Nazareth, who was a Prophet mighty in deed and word before God and all the people, and how the chief priests and our rulers delivered Him to be condemned to death, and crucified Him. But we were hoping that it was He who was going to redeem Israel" (Luke 24:17 – 21).

Our redemption was accomplished! It was Jesus who gave all people the ability to be redeemed. That is to become right with God. This was told to Abraham back in Genesis as one of the three promises received from God (see Gen.22:18).

Later, while Jesus was still with the disciples, He said,

"These are the words which I spoke to you while I was still with you, that all things must be fulfilled which were written in the Law of Moses and the Prophets and the Psalms concerning Me." And Jesus opened their understanding that they might comprehend the scriptures. Jesus then said, "Thus is written, and thus it was necessary for the Christ to suffer and to rise from the dead the third day and that repentance and remission of sins should be preached in His name to all nations, beginning at Jerusalem. And you are witnesses of these things. Behold, I send the Promise of My Father upon you; but tarry in the city of Jerusalem until you are endued with power from on high" (Luke 24:44 – 49).

"Now it came to pass, while He blessed them, that He was parted from them and carried up into heaven and they worshiped Him, and returned to Jerusalem with great joy and were continually in the temple praising and blessing God" (Luke 24:51 – 53).

What a great faith! This is the joy we should have, knowing our God has made it possible for us to be with Him! If only we knew! Now, read your Bible that you may understand. For us to get back to God, we must repent and have our sins remised (Acts 2:38).

At the crucifixion of our Lord, there were two criminals hanging on either side of Him. There was one who mocked Jesus upon the cross, suffering the same condemnation of death. But the other criminal rebuked the first, saying,

> "Do you not even fear God, seeing you are under the same condemnation? And we indeed justly, for we receive the due reward of our deeds; but this Man has done nothing wrong." Then the criminal "said to Jesus, Lord, remember me when You come into Your kingdom." And Jesus said to him, "Assuredly, I say to you, today you will be with Me in Paradise" (Luke 23:40 – 43).

As this example shows us, instead of reviling what we do not know or understand, we should live to be understanding. We need to respect the authority of God. The one criminal was understanding and sought refuge. But most of us are as the other criminal who rebuked our Lord. This is why we suffer. We suffer because we refuse to acknowledge our Lord and do not understand that all God desires from us is our obedience to Him. We do not understand because we are unwilling to listen, learn and do what it takes to obey our Lord; to repent of our sins, and to submit ourselves to growing in understanding how to live in the Spirit of God. We need to learn, but we are caught in the thorns of the deceit we are thrown into and we do not change.

What Jesus did is known throughout the entire world and is not a secret. The facts of what happened in those days are still with us. Jesus lived, died, and was buried, to be raised in newness of life, never to see corruption (see Psalm 16:10). Jesus did this willingly for us! Jesus did this so that when we hear the message of salvation He came to give, we could be with our Lord and our God in the Paradise of God, the Kingdom of God (see John 3:5).

Jesus came to give us this way. All we need to do is accept the terms He has put forth for us so that we may be with our Lord in Paradise. You may say all we need to do is believe in our God and we will have our salvation, but this is incorrect. Jesus is God and He saves those who come to Him, as He has said—not as you have said.

Therefore, I have written this story for the purpose of instruction. For us to get back to the Kingdom of God, we must do as our Lord has said. That is everyone. We must understand that Jesus's message is consistent and does not waver. "Seek first the Kingdom of God and His righteousness and all these things shall be added to you" (Matt. 6:33). But this is the seeking most are not willing to do.

What I have written is for those who want to know God. I did not write for those who say they already know God. (Though most could learn from what I present). I wrote for all who desire to find the way to be with God in His Kingdom—if, in fact, you desire to know this even exists! It seems to be easy, but most will not understand that being with God requires a change be made. The change you make needs to be in accordance with what God has given.

I have come a long way in the life I have been given to understand the gift of love our Lord has bestowed upon us. Especially after being married and still not getting it right. I have made sacrifices and thought little of my worldly wealth as I lived to find God and lead my family to Him. I took on the monumental task of building my faith in a world that measures your stature according to the amount of worldly success you have. I am conquering my lack of belief by trusting what God has said.

Though I point out the blatant sin of those who, willingly or unwillingly, walk outside of what God has given to us, I do not do so because I hate those people. I point out the sin of those who walk contrary to the Word of God so that we may learn and understand it is God who has made right and wrong. I am simply a messenger.

I hope you will heed what God has given through what has been written about holy men and women—and not-so-holy men and women—in the past. I am not miraculously inspired by God to be a messenger, but I have decided to teach what I know. I have learned about God by reading God's Word and you can too. My goal is to help our world understand we all must serve our God, according to what we have as it is written.

Thank you for reading this book.

1

What You Need to Know

IN THE BEGINNING of His ministry, Jesus our Lord said very clearly to the Pharisee Nicodemus that there is only one way to get back to the kingdom of God (see John 3.5). Make no mistakes based on what you have been told concerning what our Lord has given. The instructions Jesus gave to Nicodemus are imperative for all, and they cannot be changed by anyone. Who can change what God has given? Who has this authority to speak on behalf of God or to tell God He needs to change? Jesus our Lord gave instructions to us we have no authority to change. So I am writing to inform you concerning what our Lord has given.

> "There was a man of the Pharisees named Nicodemus, a ruler of the Jews. This man came to Jesus by night and said to Him, "Rabbi, we know that You are a teacher come from God; for no one can do these signs that You do unless God is with him."

> Jesus answered and said to him, "Most assuredly, I say to you unless one is born again, he cannot see the kingdom of God."

> Nicodemus said to Him, "How can a man be born when he is old? Can he enter a second time into his mother's womb and be born?"
>
> Jesus answered, "Most assuredly, I say to you, unless one is born of water and the Spirit, he cannot enter the kingdom of God" (John 3:1–5).

I am a man who was baptized to die to sin to be raised in newness of life. As it is recorded in John 3, when we are baptized into Christ's death, it is a certainty that we who have died to sin should not live any longer in sin (see Rom. 6). After baptism, our purpose needs to be renewing our minds to God (see Rom. 12:2). That is, we need to repent in our walk of life to live as God would have us live. Acts 2:38 is a perfect example of this truth. Thousands accepted what Jesus instructed the apostles, and Peter delivered to the masses gathered on Pentecost. Peter and the other apostles did what our Lord instructed, and we need to as well if we desire to be in the Kingdom of our Lord.

If we do not repent, our baptism will mean nothing. This is because we will not be walking within the Spirit that God desires us to walk within. Therefore, we will lose what we thought we could obtain, for the simple reason we have disobeyed the commandment of God. Remember, it was Jesus who said, "If you love Me, keep My commandments" (John 14:15). If you continue to live as you have always done, ignoring what Jesus has said, you by definition do not love God. Like the Jewish leaders of the time of Christ, you do not consider yourself worthy of eternal life (see Acts 13:46). Clearly, most people have not given this much thought. The old adage "what you do not see will not hurt you" applies here. But that does not apply here. Ignorance is not a state of bliss! Perhaps you have not heard about Jesus! What then? Considering all of the religious and political noise in the world, it is not a stretch to believe that to be true. That is what makes it even more imperative we actually search for the things of God when we are even slightly interested in God. You cannot serve God according to your own desires and expect to be right with God.

Because I sought to know God, a way of understanding was made known to me. By understanding and through reason of what the Scripture of God teaches, I have striven to live my life in the Spirit as God has instructed, so I can be right with God. This way of living has taken me some time to learn, and I have struggled because of my lack of self-control, but I have learned to grow in what our Lord commanded. I have learned to lean upon how God would have me live. I do my best to live the life I should. I do my best to help those whom I know and love, as well as those whom I do not know, to understand how important our lives are to God and our need to live as God desires us to understand.

If this means nothing to you now, then you have some reading to do and understanding to grasp, just as I did. Pick up a Bible from somewhere and study. The context of all our lives needs to build upon the understanding that God is first in all things. So I live as I should, in accordance with the Spirit God desires us to have as much as is within me (Romans 8). Thank God for baptism!

We will speak about baptism later, but by this time, I hope you are beginning to understand what Jesus meant when He said, "Born of water and the Spirit." By understanding, I do not hold to the doctrine and desires of men concerning what God has given. Granted, this is very tricky, with all of the false teaching going on today about our God. However, you can come to the correct understanding of what God has given to us if you look at what God has said instead of what false teachers teach. We need to grasp this basic understanding. It remains elusive, but only because people do not read what God has given and grow their faith in God.

We all can know God's Word, and we need to. But there are those who do not hold to God's Word in the correct manner and speak things which are not true. They wish to impose their manner of life upon those of us who do want to serve God correctly and most are caught up in this error. They espouse erroneous interpretations of what God's Word says concerning the way our lives are to be. These people, whom I would call progressives, are wrong. They confuse others and do so for generations to come. Let me give you some examples:

1. *We can never lose our salvation.* This claim is patently false. Israel lost their salvation and Jesus said, "Anyone does not abide in Me, he is cast out as a branch and is withered; and they gather them and throw them into the fire, and they are burned" (John 15:6). If you refuse to repent, this is you. This is why Israel was cast away. Don't forget about Adam and Eve.

2. *Homosexuality is accepted by God.* This is another false teaching. Homosexuality is a sin, and "unless you repent you will all likewise perish" (Luke 13:5). Again, this is simply because you are not abiding in God. Consider Romans 1:24–32 as well.

3. *Adultery and sexual promiscuity are not sins.* The description in 1 Corinthians 6:9–11 paints a different picture. These will not inherit the kingdom of God:

   - Fornicators
   - Idolaters
   - Adulterers
   - Homosexuals
   - Thieves
   - Coveters
   - Drunkards
   - Revilers
   - Extortioners

4. *Marriage, divorce, and remarriage are not wrong.* Jesus says, "But I say to you that whoever divorces his wife for any reason except sexual immorality causes her to commit adultery; and whoever marries a woman who is divorced commits adultery" (Matt. 5:32). Again, "And I say to you, whoever divorces his wife, except for sexual immorality, and marries another, commits adultery; and whoever marries her who is divorced commits adultery" (Matt. 19:9).

5. *It is not a problem to lie.* Lying is also against the sound doctrine of God. "The law is not made for a righteous person, but the lawless and insubordinate for the ungodly and sinners, for the unholy and profane, for murderers of fathers and murderers of mothers, for manslayers, for fornicators, for sodomites, for kidnappers, for liars, for perjurers, and if there is any other thing that is contrary to sound doctrine" (1 Tim. 1:9–11).

Just these five ways of living people hold to are a major part of what has destroyed our ability to understand what God has given to us. These five beliefs are what have set our world on end. We believe we are the end of all reason and justify what we do based on what our desires are.

Living a life contrary to what God has said is going against what naturally goes together and is wrong. Ignorance of God is against humanity. God created us, and we all need to know God. The good of our lives depends upon our knowing God.

As a student of God's Word, I see what God has given to us and our subsequent need to reconcile our lives to God. This is why I have written about coming back to the Kingdom of God. I have learned of our need to reconcile our lives to God by reading and understanding what God has provided for us. I have seen it with my own eyes. I have not relied on what others tell me concerning God unless what they tell me concurs 100 percent with what I can read in God's Word. Clearly, God's Word says we all need to reconcile our lives to Him.

Understand that we all need to get back to the Kingdom of God if we do not want the other option. Look to all of the chaos around us today for a glimpse of what your future will be if you do not come to God. I hope you will be able to see your need to put the way of God first in your life and ignore the popular teachers, like Joel Osteen or Billy Graham, who do not teach the gospel according to the truth of God. Their teaching is a "doctrine of demons" (1 Tim. 4:1), which is an application of Matthew 4:1–11. For instance, our salvation requires more than saying a prayer, believing, and confessing. Read your Bible to know the truth.

You can see that I make references to the Word of God. The Word of our God holds the keys to the Kingdom of God (see Matt. 16:19). So I give you passages of Scripture to reference, and I will also quote what the Word of God actually says. It would be a good thing to have your Bible close by so you may understand what has been written for our learning and verify what I say as true or not. Believe the Word of God and not those who preach and teach words not supported by what God has given to us. Please ask me questions and I would be glad to answer them: Bill at bmxbooks@gmail.com.

Importantly, I have reiterated certain verses from our Lord Jesus Christ because what He has said, as recorded by the writers of the gospel, is essential to our understanding the context of what God has given to us through His Son, so that we can get back to the Kingdom of God.

One of those verses is John 3:5: "Jesus answered, 'Most assuredly, I say to you, unless one is born of water and the Spirit, he cannot enter the kingdom of God.'"

This is basic understanding, but elusive because most do not investigate what God's Word actually says. God's Word is the Truth. But those who do not know God may not be able to comprehend what has been prepared for our learning as being true. This is simply because they are unwilling to or just have not read God's Word.

It could also be that those who do not know God have been so indoctrinated by their liberal or humanistic mindset, denomination, or other false teachings that they cannot see the actual truth of what God has given to us. Understanding who God is requires faith, and you cannot have faith in God unless you know God (see Hebrews 11). Unless people have been grounded in the truth of what God has given to us, they will not understand God or will have a difficult time with what their faith in God should be. This is simply because there are too many distractions.

Discerning the truth of God is not impossible—in fact, it is easy! But you must build your faith in God, which is difficult if not impossible if you refuse to look to God and what He has given to us. When you refuse to study what the Scriptures say the trusting faith you can have of our God will be far from you (see 2 Tim. 2:15). Remember, the Bible was written for our learning (Rom. 15.4) so finding what God desires from His people is not impossible. I have done it, and I came from zero understanding of what God has given to us. It was not until I was twenty-four years old that I began to put together the way of God. I did this because I was searching. I was looking to God's Word, and I obeyed. Therefore, I know "faith without works is dead" (James 2:17).

Essential to our faith in God is actually knowing God. I hope you also understand there is an adversary who is always against us. This adversary is Satan. Satan is the reason we are where we are today. As I have read, he is the source of our division. It seems kind of ridiculous to think we have an adversary who is constantly working against our relationship with God and each other, but this is a true statement. Satan is and always has been our adversary. Satan is the reason we miss the mark God desires us to attain.

Most people are confused about who God is. Those who do not look to what God has given for our learning do not realize we are fighting against what God has given to us, to the point we think there is no God and any religion is okay. The adversary is the reason we struggle to know right and wrong and refuse to listen to what God has prepared for our learning. As I understand, Satan and our weak volition are the reasons we doubt.

Most of the time, the Word of God is passed up as just another story. A lot of people do not realize the words contained in the Bible are what guide us away from being eternally lost. The newness and pleasures of life—worldly opportunities, political associations, and various religions—take over our desires. This has an overreaching opportunity cost for all, as our actions influence others to walk outside of what God has given to us.

A persistent question may arise in our minds about people being able to make any decision they would like. Sadly, most do not know God. They think anything they desire to do and any idea they have about who God is would be fine. This is not the case. God is not who we make Him out to be. God is who He has said He is and He has given us instructions we are to live by. This is what the Bible is for. God has made His way known to us, but even in this we have rejected Him.

The Bible is clear: God is first in all things, and we need to place Him there (see Matt. 6:33). There is right and wrong, and God is always right. God wants us to know Him, but we do not, and that is problematic.

The truth is, we left what God has given to us beginning in the garden of Eden, and God has let us believe the manifestations of our intent. This is not what God gave us, but what we desired. Life has become what we desire, which takes us away from our God—unless it is God whom we desire, according to the Spirit He has given to us. Simply read the Bible for confirmation. Remember and read Romans 8 for clarification. At this point in life instead of knowing God and what His will is for us, what we desire is confusion under the guise of "our rights." We contrive rights where none exist. We seek to justify everyone being right in their own eyes. Look to Judges 21:25 for why this is wrong. Even some brethren are swept away in this, especially when it comes to their children. This is quite the opposite of what God has given to us and is very detrimental to the health of our world. We can see this every day. Now I am not speaking of racial equality, but rather when a man desires to change into a woman simply because this is the way he feels. The implications of this becoming a right will drive the people of the world even further away from God. Are you beginning to see how Satan has affected us? The only difference is we do not see Satan in the form of a serpent.

Today it is essential that we find God before it is too late. This book is my attempt to help you see where you fit in. What is paramount in our understanding is that God has given many good things to us. The adversary is the one who is constantly taking the good away. He has even taken away our belief which leads to faith in God.

Don't get me wrong; we willingly gave up what God has given to us, for the purpose of believing a lie. God will let us do this when we do not care to understand who God is or what He has given for us. The passage 2 Thessalonians 2:9–11 explains this application of Genesis 3. The serpent deceived Eve, and she believed the lie. You see, God did not create robots to move at His will, as some false religions will teach you. God made us so we could make decisions and live within the context of what He gave to us. God gave us Paradise and we lost it because Adam and Eve did not trust God enough to ignore the serpent. Neither do we. As time has gone on, we have simply gone further from God and ignored what has been for our learning (see Rom. 15:4).

What God has chosen to reveal to us is what we have for our learning. It is what we need to know as we strive to live our lives (see Deut. 29:29). The Word of God is the truth of our lives and we must not ignore it.

This, however, is what we do because we do not care to know the Word of God. Instead, we let the activities of life supersede

9

what we should know, simply because we do not know any differently. Ever since man and woman were removed from the garden of Eden, our lack of understanding has been our problem. Even so, no matter what you may have heard or understood, the Word of God tells us of God's love, grace, and mercy. The Bible also tells us of God's justice. In fact, God demands justice and will punish those who misuse justice (see Mic. 6:8). Keep this within your thoughts at all times. God will repay those who commit evil (see Rom. 12:17-21). The Bible is the story of our beginning, and we need to know it.

Remember, what we consider to be right is not always right. More often than not what people desire is selfish and wrong, unless it is according to the knowledge of what God has given to us. What we consider to be our enlightened desires are not what our Lord has given to us. The sad truth is people are mostly selfish and do not seek the things of God, nor do they desire the protection God is willing to give us. Read and consider what Satan said to Eve in the garden and her response in Genesis 3:

> "Now the serpent was more cunning than any
> beast of the field which the Lord God had made.
> And he said to the woman, "Has God indeed said,
> 'You shall not eat of every tree of the garden'?"
>
> And the woman said to the serpent, "We may eat
> the fruit of the trees of the garden; but of the fruit
> of the tree which *is* in the midst of the garden,
> God has said, 'You shall not eat it, nor shall you
> touch it, lest you die.'"
>
> Then the serpent said to the woman, "You will
> not surely die. For God knows that in the day you
> eat of it your eyes will be opened, and you will be
> like God, knowing good and evil."

"So when the woman saw that the tree *was* good for food, that it *was* pleasant to the eyes, and a tree desirable to make *one* wise, she took of its fruit and ate. She also gave to her husband with her, and he ate. Then the eyes of both of them were opened, and they knew that they *were* naked; and they sewed fig leaves together and made themselves coverings."

Are you beginning to see what I am saying?

Instead of how it was before the sin of Adam and Eve, it is we now need to renew our minds to God, even though we do not care to. Since our enlightenment, we are not willing to accept that which God has given to us. This is because we have "progressed" all the way to a lack of faith, even with God's Word in front of us! I do not mean this to be taken the wrong way, but if you consider your life and the lives of those around you, most people are simply unfaithful and unwilling participants in abiding in God. I wish all people considered God first in their day-to-day activities, but this simply does not happen. Sin is the reason.

According to the Word of God, God gave us life and continues to let us live by reason of His unstoppable grace that few will take advantage of. Today, because of our progress, living for God is almost an impossible task. Our collective unbelief in God continues to grow. But I hope after reading what I have prepared, you will understand why your thinking needs to change. I hope you will make God first in your every consideration. When you do this, the manifestations of your intent will be successful! Just put God where He belongs! Make God first in your life! This is how we get back to His Kingdom!

Regardless of what we believe, we are all in the same boat. I believe we desire to help each other see how to live better, but this is based in the improvements we create. Why not live as God would have us live? We do not live as God desires because we refuse to look to the basic commandments of our God for understanding. We hold to man contrived standards and seek to justify ourselves by ourselves. Most people do not love God. We covet things that take our devotion away from God. Loving our God and loving our neighbor as ourselves is very far from us (see Matt. 22:34 – 40). We need to put God first.

Last but not least, none of us is perfect. We all have our struggles. I know I have many. However, I study to know the Word of God. Given my imperfection, I want to let you know that I understand what it is not to believe in God. I understand we all have questions about God and why we should believe in Him. I also know we should know our Lord and Savior by taking the time to learn about Him. For this to happen though, we need to recognize when we do not know Him. We cannot let what we have created keep us from understanding God. Our Lord was tempted as a man (albeit at a different time), tried just as we are, but was without sin. He knows our struggles and He knows God. The problem is we do not know our Lord and our God.

2

The Kingdom of God

NOW LET ME help you fix this: I have learned about God by reading the historical truths written in the Bible.

In the beginning of all life, God gave us a perfect world. God gave us a garden Paradise. We had God before us and all was good (see Gen. 1:31). There was nothing amiss in the garden Paradise (Kingdom) of God until what God created desired to walk outside of what God had given. This was to fulfill the desire of the adversary (see Gen. 3). What this created is what we have today.

As the created of God, we were given Paradise to tend. What God created was good and there was nothing created that was not good until we decided to walk away from God. In creation, all things were built by God (see Heb. 3:4). According to Scripture, people had an ability to make a choice. As the created of God, we could choose to do right or we could choose to do wrong (see Gen. 4:7). Such are we, who chose to walk adversely to what God has given for us to live according to His will. Over time this error has just become our manner of living and we do not know any differently. This is only because we have "progressed" from being able to acknowledge God. Therefore, we do not believe God exists.

In Genesis 3, we see how the serpent tempted Eve away from God and Adam immediately joined her. It was at this point mankind walked away from God and the Paradise we were given to tend. Instead of staying with God man pursued his desires and though warning us to repent, God did not stop us. Our reliance on self had taken over. At this point, we had to learn how to keep ourselves close to God while managing all of our daily tasks that became necessary for us to survive.

Why did this happen? Why did the serpent live adversely to what God gave and seek to bring us with him? Why walk away from the good of God for the purpose of leading others astray? What good could possibly be gained by this? Nothing! That is nothing but selfish ambition with a desire to deceive. This is when evil took over.

The Word of God does not explicitly give us an indication as to why the serpent desired to be contrary to what God created except that he did. As I have read, the serpent was just that way. However, because of what was and is our inability to trust what God has given to us, we have had to struggle to come back to God. We now need to labor for our provision and we have progressed all the way to unbelief in God.

What God gave was good, and what woman and man decided to do was not in accordance with what God had given. We now live according to the deceit of the adversary of God. Because of this, our desires are not combined with the knowledge of God and cause us to fall short. Most do not understand this.

This is simple to understand, right?

When you do what God says not to do, this is not being empowered. Going against God is going against His authority and enslaving ourselves to our own manner of living. We all can see how this has gone. But even as life has gone outside of God's provision in the garden, because of God's enduring grace and mercy, we still have time to reconcile our lives to God (see Eph. 2:4 – 10). Unfortunately, as time has gone on, we do not recognize our need to be reconciled according to God and we misuse the grace God has given to us. We fail to see our need to be reconciled to God according to God. We fail to see the totality of Jesus, who came "to be sin for us that we might become the righteousness of God in Him" (2 Cor. 5:20). Most believe Jesus death removed our responsibility to obey our God and this is wrong.

As long as we are alive, we still have the ability to learn, turn back to God, and be the good God created. The grace of God is still here and God is not willing that any should perish. But we need to be partakers of the grace God has given by doing the will of God (see 2 Peter 3:9).

The apostle Paul told the Philippians this very thing. The Philippians had fellowship with Paul because they believed in Jesus Christ. Therefore, because of what Paul taught according to Jesus Christ, the Philippians as well as others described in the Bible, these are our examples of how to live according to the grace of our God. Learning how we get back to the Kingdom of God is what the New Testament is for.

But even with the simplicity of understanding we all can have about who God is, what we mostly do not comprehend is a healthy respect for God and what He has given to us. We believe we can make God into whomever we desire as we ignore the Bible or change it to fit our notions. Our love and care for God is very misdirected.

We struggle to understand or plainly do not comprehend that our God ultimately gave us a Kingdom to tend to. When we walked away from the garden Paradise, God remained close to us because of His grace. God has given us an eternal sacrifice we can be part of when we obey (see John 14:15). This understanding of who God is has become lost as we have left God for our own reasoning. God has given us over to ourselves, to do those things "which are not fitting" (Rom. 1:28). A lot of people know this, but choose not to do anything about it. These are those who deny God exists and have done so of their own accord. Israel is a perfect example, yet, so is my neighbor who I am to love as myself. God does not force His way upon anyone, but He does let those who will, as I have pointed out to you, believe the lie (see 2 Thess. 2:11).

Just so you know, Israel desired an earthly king to rule over them and God gave them what they desired (see end of Judges, Samuel, Kings, and Chronicles). But then God also gave Israel a heavenly King and Israel rejected Him (see Matthew, Mark, Luke and John). The heavenly King, Jesus would lead them to God, but Israel did not believe. Why? Tradition? Desire?

Remember that it was Israel who disobeyed Moses, God's servant, whose task was to lead them to know God and reach the land flowing with milk and honey (see Ex. 3:17). This was a paradise on the earth, but Israel was unwilling to believe in God. Israel walked away from what God had promised. God did not.

Today, I contend, most people do not care what God has given to us. Out of ignorance and for various other reasons, people do not even consider all of the greatness of what God has done. As I embark on this journey of helping all who read what I have written to know the Kingdom of God and our need to come back to the Kingdom God has given to us, I encourage you to take the time to learn about our God and what He has given to us in His Word. For example, the term "kingdom" is defined in the same way in every instance we look at.

1. In the Hebrew: *mamlakah* (Strong's H4467)—dominion, estate, country where one is sovereign[1]
2. In the Greek: *basileia* (Strong's G932)—the territory subject to the rule of a king[2]

---

[1] Strong, James; Vine, W.E., *The New Strong's Concise Concordance* & Vines Concise Dictionary of the Bible (Nashville: Thomas Nelson, 1997, 1999), 207.

[2] Strong, James; Vine, W.E. The New Strong's Concise Concordance & Vines Concise Dictionary of the Bible (Nashville: Thomas Nelson, 1997, 1999), 207.

3. Internet search: *kingdom*—a country, state, or territory ruled by a king or a queen; the spiritual reign or authority of God

So a kingdom is an area over which a king has authority. This is simple to understand, right? But who is God?

In the Hebrew, we look to God and can see His names are far too wonderful for us. This lack of comprehension is because of who we have become, of our own accord. God speaks to Moses in Exodus 3, and Moses asks God His name. "And God said to Moses, 'I AM WHO I AM'" (see Ex. 3:14). I contend that we simply do not comprehend this greatness because we do not comprehend all that God is to us. It should go without saying, then, that the names of God are far greater than I am able to give to you, except what I can know according to the Scripture of God.

For this time, suffice it to say there are many different ways to describe God in the Hebrew, based on His characteristics. Looking at the Hebrew word *Elohim*, we see this means God: ruler and judge who created the world. According to a word search, I have found "God" in this form occurs 2,606 times in the Old Testament.

Elohim is the plural of *Eloah*, which also means God and occurs 57 times in the Bible. *Eloah* comes from the root word *el* and occurs in the Hebrew Bible 235 times. It also means God or godlike, mighty, and power.

Taking the root one step further, *el* comes from *ayil*, which means ram and other terms conveying strength. *Ayil* occurs 185 times in the Old Testament. Ultimately *Elohim* is from *uwl*, also meaning mighty and strength. It occurs twice in the Hebrew Bible.

Consider this: in Hebrew, the letter aleph signifies God. Anciently speaking, aleph was the ox head used by Israel to indicate God. If you were to see and understand the meaning of who God is as the Hebrew language tells us, I believe you would see a much larger picture than what I am giving you. As the called of God, Israel had God before them at all times until they left God for their own way. For that matter, Adam and Eve had God in their midst, but there is no accounting of any written languages from that time, and we do not see any of the way Adam and Eve thought except what Moses wrote.

Let it be known that God is known to us, regardless of what has been conjured in the minds of those who do not believe that we have always had the revelation of God. Yet, even with this truth, we continually go further and further away from the One who created us and gave us Paradise to live in. We have modernized ourselves so far away from God that we rarely ever comprehend what God has given us and what He is waiting to give us if we will only obey Him. As a result of our disobedience, God has given us over to survive according to the desires of who and what we have become. As we embrace new technologies giving us new ways of living, it would be prudent to make certain God is embraced first. Otherwise, we will slip further and further away from God.

This is why I am writing to you now. This is why I am telling you about God and our need to come back to Him. Growing up, I never knew God. This was what my parents and society had created for me. Once I learned of God I have lived to change this. Up until I was 24 year old, no one I knew believed in God as God has given. Our ancestors left their responsibility of teaching us who God is. Because of what life had become, they did not focus on God. If we were to obey God, we would have singularity of thought, and life would be better. Be understanding.

Obedience is the key. When we get back to His Kingdom through our obedience to God's authority, then we will behold this amazing time. Until then, the chaos continues and people continue to create ways and processes that are right to them when they do not even know what is right or clearly know how to govern these processes or people correctly. In this, people continue to say there is no need for obedience to God because God has given us His mercy and grace, or because they erroneously believe God does not exist. I tell you God does exist. God has given us His mercy and grace. But this is to allow us time to reconcile ourselves to God (see 2 Cor. 5:20). But because of this grace we have been given, we instead ignore God.

Today, after Jesus has nailed the old Law to the cross (see Col. 2:14), we need to be born of water and the Spirit to enter the Kingdom God is waiting to give us where Jesus is King. We need to be a part of that Kingdom if we desire to be with God (see John 3:5). To do otherwise is not wise, as you are walking outside of what God has given. Do not mistake me, God has always desired we walk within the Spirit He has.

So what has God given to us? God created Paradise for us. God created us and placed us within the perfect environment of His Kingdom upon this earth. God placed us within the garden of Eden. He even gave us the ability to reason and make choices. Contrary to popular teachings, we all have free will unless we have been held captive for some reason, those reasons being countless and due in every way to human activity. So, God is not the source of our problems. Our problems stem from the adversary of God, the selfish ambition of men and women, and the indoctrination of children by those who lack the understanding God desires all to have. We have left the single most important responsibility we need to fulfill in our lives, and it all began with Adam and Eve falling for what the adversary deceived us with.

Adam and Eve were given Paradise to cultivate. Within the garden paradise there were two trees that were very significant among all of the other plants and animals Adam and Eve lived with. These two trees were the Tree of Life (Gen. 2:9, 3:22) and the Tree of the Knowledge of Good and Evil (Gen. 2:9, 3:1–24).

Within this perfect environment, God instructed, "Of the tree of the knowledge of good and evil you shall not eat, for in the day that you eat of it you shall surely die" (Gen. 2:17). But eat

Adam and Eve did. They walked outside of what God gave to them because they gave in to temptation. Eve believed the lie of the one who would deceive her, the serpent. But what has God done for us since! Read your Bible!

I could write a lot more about what God has given to us, but I will try to keep this brief and simple to understand. Since removing mankind from the garden of Eden, God has been merciful to us. God's mercy remained with Adam, but God gave Adam what he desired. Adam was able to remain with Eve outside of the garden, but they had to work for their sustenance—something that was not so difficult before. God was still with them, but God removed Adam and Eve from the Paradise we had be given.

Adam and Eve, because of the mercy God has for all, had time to reconcile their lives to God. It's the same for us. Remember, God is the King, and He has given us a place to live continually within His Kingdom. Your lack of understanding does not change this fact. In fact, the man God gave to be the second king of Israel (David) recognized the earth and all who dwell within it are the Lord's, and we should do the same (see Ps. 24:1).

God was among us in the garden of Eden, but since the time of our removal, God has chosen to communicate with those who are willing and able to convey the message God has given to His people. At least this is how I see what has been written. Thus, you have the lineage of people given in the Word of God for our learning up to our Lord and Savior, who is our final offering for the sins we commit.

But ever since the first sin, there has been a need to have our sins remised. We can see this need with the example of Cain and Abel. They needed to offer sacrifices to God to be right with God. Therefore, God requires us to offer something of value according to His instructions for us to be right with Him; from Adam and Eve to the ultimate offering for sin through Jesus Christ, God's Son. We need to let go of our pride! God has given us the ability to understand this fact: we left God because of our desires that were not in accordance with what God has given. We have mostly been able to reason the way of God in our lives. Instead, we chose to listen to deceitful words and justify our desires.

But even so, God has continued to give us His grace. He has shown us favor and we who serve God as God is, we live and learn to have respect and adoration for God ever more as we grow. We are those who do not forget to share because this is well pleasing to God (see Heb. 13:16). Men and women for thousands of years have lived with this ability to know what God has given to us, but we have not reciprocated in the same manner. Because some do actually heed what God has said, God has shown what is good and what He requires of us. God has given us the ability to comprehend and "do justly, to love mercy, and to walk humbly with our God" (Mic. 6:8). God has given us the ability to know "all things that pertain to life and Godliness, through the knowledge of Him who called us by glory and virtue," that through these we "may be partakers of the divine nature, having escaped the corruption that is in the world through lust" (2 Pet. 1:3, 4).

It is this grace and understanding which has been given to us today by God through Jesus Christ our Lord. It is that we have written for our learning (Rom. 15:4) that God has continued to give us "precious promises" (see 2 Pet. 1:4). Even as we have been given the promise of life, we must also grow in faith in our God and in the knowledge of our Lord Jesus Christ. It is because of the favor God has toward what He has created that we have the ability to come back to God. "For it is by grace we have been saved through faith and that not of yourselves, grace is a gift from God" (Eph. 2:8).

We live because of the grace God has shown to us. He has given us mercy, such that we are brought near to God by the sacrificial blood of Christ (see Eph. 2:13). It is Christ's blood that saves us because we are justified by His blood even as enemies (see Col. 1:21). We are reconciled to God through the blood of Jesus by being born of water and the Spirit (see Rom. 5:9, 10; Rom. 6; Eph. 5:10; John 3:5).

But here is the problem. We the people are not able to reconcile what God has given to us—that we must buried with Christ in order to be right with God. Instead, we erroneously think the grace of God means we do not have to obey God. Read Romans chapters 5 and 6. You cannot take one chapter and ignore the other. If Paul was told "what he must do" (Acts 9:6) by our Lord, and he tells us the same thing, are we any different that we can ignore the basic command to be baptized (Acts 9:18)? "For as by one man's disobedience many were made sinners, so also by one Man's obedience many will be made righteous" (Rom. 5:19).

In this, God has given us His Son. For us to be reconciled to God, we must understand how to be reconciled. "Therefore we are buried with Him through baptism into death, that just as Christ was raised from the dead by the glory of the Father, even so we also should walk in newness of life" (Rom. 6:4).

Baptism and living in the Spirit of God is how we are reconciled. God has given us the ability to come to Him through the offering of His Son as the final sacrifice for sin. When we obey God, then we will be buried with Christ through baptism, to be raised as a new person in the "likeness of His resurrection" (Rom. 6:5). This is how we live in the Kingdom of God and congregate with the brethren.

We have been given the promise of life with God, to live with Him back in the Paradise He is willing to give to us. But we must be willing to become "slaves of God" to take part in everlasting life (Rom. 6:22).

We sinned by our own desires and God removed us from Paradise. We no longer had eternal life. Now all die. This may seem harsh, but God is King and God makes the rules. We do not make the rules. God is "not willing that any should perish but that all should come to repentance" (2 Pet. 3:9). This too is according to His rules. We need to reconcile ourselves to God (see 2 Cor. 5:20). We must be willing to "grow in the grace and knowledge of our Lord and Savior Jesus Christ" (2 Pet. 3:18). This acknowledgment is our choice.

Only when we acknowledge what God has said will we be able to understand all God has done for us. We need to change our lives and live as God has given us the ability to live. "For none of us lives to himself, and no one dies to himself. For if we live, we live to the Lord; and if we die, we die to the Lord. Therefore, whether we live or die, we are the Lord's" (Rom. 14:7–8).

Though God has freely given us His Son, His Son has given us instructions as recorded in the gospels we need to follow. He gave us this guidance so we may come back to God. Remember, unless you are born of water and the Spirit, you cannot enter the Kingdom of God.

3

Christ is King

AS CHRIST IS the King (see Heb. 1:1-14), we enter into the Kingdom He established by doing His will (John 14:15). The gospels tell us Jesus is King and for this reason Jesus was crucified (see Matt. 27:11). Today, our understanding begins with our knowing that Jesus died for all and was raised in newness of life for the purpose of our salvation. Paul writes:

> "For I am not ashamed of the gospel of Christ, for it is the power of God to salvation for everyone who believes, for the Jew first and also for the Greek." (Romans 1:16).

When we have done as Jesus instructed in John 3.5 we are added to the Kingdom of the Son. The church our Lord gave His life for exists independent of what anyone would like to say. Our Lord established His church as a congregation of people gathered in His name. "For as many of you as were baptized into Christ have put on Christ" (Gal. 3:27). As Christ has all authority then it only makes sense that when we are baptized we are to live by His rule (see Matt. 28:18-20). As we live according to His rule then we are in His Kingdom.

The gospels tell the story of our Lord, and the book of Acts establishes without a doubt the church belongs to Christ. When we gather together in church on Sunday to worship, we gather in the name of the Lord. If your congregation does not ascribe its establishment, name, or teachings to Christ our Lord, you by definition are not in the Lord's church.

Most people do not respect our need for salvation from the eternal damnation we will encounter because of what the adversary initially caused as recorded in Genesis 3. Certainly, most people do not know or respect that "there is no other name under heaven given among men by which we must be saved" (Acts 4:12). In fact, this knowledge of our Lord has been hidden and neglected because people choose to do what is right in their own eyes. Knowledge of God's Son has been kept from a lot of people simply because of negligence and inaction. The gospel of God has even been forcibly removed by threats of violence and acts leading to the death of those who would proclaim salvation in Christ and no other. The threats come from many different places. As the people God created for His purpose, we are way past the point of not understanding that God needs to be first in our lives. Knowing God is far from us, and this because of how we have built our lives.

Paul says, "For if we live, we live to the Lord; and if we die, we die to the Lord. Therefore, whether we live or die, we are the Lord's" (Rom. 14:8). In another place it is written, "And if you are Christ's, then you are Abraham's seed and heirs according to the promise" (Gal. 3:29). Why is this? Do you remember the promise given to Abraham? It was through Abraham's seed all the nations of the earth will be blessed. We need to understand we all belong to the Lord, no matter what we believe. This begins with our understanding.

In due time, our Lord "gave Himself for us, that He might redeem us from every lawless deed and purify for Himself His own special people zealous for good works" (Titus 2:14). Our Lord "suffered once for sins, the just for the unjust that He might bring us to God, being put to death in the flesh, but alive in the Spirit" (1 Pet. 3:18). Remember John 3:5 says unless you are born of water and the Spirit, you cannot enter the Kingdom of God.

This is the problem though. Not a lot of people are zealous for good works. Most people have very little respect for our Lord. Our problem is that we do not comprehend what Jesus has done for us because ultimately, we do not care to. We do not believe that knowledge of Jesus is vital to our existence and we make the church and God into whatever we deem as correct. My experience has told me most people just do not know who we are to God and learning to care about this is a daunting task to say the least. The understanding we are to have of God therefore goes unnoticed and our respect for God is lacking.

I see no end in sight to our unwillingness to come back to God. Preach and teach as we may, there are those who will always neglect their salvation for self-righteousness. A lot of people are unwilling to comprehend what it means to renew our minds to God and be born of water and the Spirit. The adversary has us right where he desires we remain. Why? As I said before, I do not know why the adversary chose to be this way. But just because I do not know does not diminish the facts we have been given in God's Word.

The Word of God tells us that the Kingdom of God is where Jesus is sitting at God's right hand (Eph. 1:22). The apostle Paul wrote that Christ is the head of the church (see Eph. 5:23–24). The church is Christ's because our Lord stated, "I will build My church" (Matt. 16:18). But even back in the first century, people were trying to ascribe the church of our Lord to others. In 1 Corinthians chapter 1, the apostle Paul says that there are heated disagreements and assertions that what Christ created and died for can be ascribed to another person. "Is Christ divided? Was Paul crucified for you? Or were you baptized in the name of Paul? I thank God that I baptized none of you except Crispus and Gaius, lest anyone should say that I had baptized in my own name" (1 Cor. 1:13-15).

The apostles whom Jesus taught ascribed the church Jesus established in His name to Jesus and so should we. The church is Christ's! The church is the body of Christ (see Eph. 5:23). It is made up of people zealous for good works born of water and the Spirit. Jesus says the church of His creation is His, as we can read in the gospels and in the book of Acts. Here we see the development of the church according to established instructions given by our Lord. Paul and the other apostles taught this very fact. Jesus taught this! The church is our Lord's according to the teachings which He gave to the apostles, as recorded in the gospels, Acts, and the letters to the Christians. We understand the church is Christ's because it was our Lord who gave the apostles the authority to teach and baptize in His name (see Matthew 28 and Luke 24). That authority was granted for the purpose of adding those who would be baptized into Christ to the church our Lord, established through His blood (see John 3.5). As those who are zealous for good works, we who desire to be a part of the church Christ established must conform to His teachings.

So ownership with regard to the church is a very important concept we must understand and not take lightly. Unfortunately, there are those who do not hold to the sound doctrine of what God, through our Lord, has given to us (see 2 Tim. 1:13). They establish practices of worship based on man-made decrees. They take what is Christ's and ascribe it to someone else, essentially invalidating our salvation in God through Christ. This is what Catholicism and denominationalism have done. This is what Islam, Hinduism and any other form of worship to a god does also. Believe as you may, but just know there is only one Truth (see Acts 4:12 & Eph. 4:5).

The principle I hope you understand is we need to believe the church is Christ's. You, I or anyone else cannot take what Christ our Lord established and call it whatever we would like.

For some reason, our understanding that Jesus Christ is the head of the church He began has gone away. It has vanished. Men and women have taken what our Lord began and made the church into whatever they desired. This is wrong and ignorant of Scripture.

My question is, why anyone would ascribe the church Christ gave His life for to someone else? Why is it that those who preach according to denominational practice do not respect the words of our Lord and hold to man-made teachings concerning our God? Sadly, denominationalists teach the doctrine of God according to the commandments of men, and this is wrong. Did man create God? Did man create a story of a people chosen by God only to be destroyed, or chosen by God for our pleasure? No.

What God has given to us is His Word and history proves this to be true. I cannot create a congregation for the purpose of worshipping our God according to my own desires, half-truths, or a college education, and call it what God desires. That is theft, and theft is wrong and a sin. Remember "Thou shall not steal" (Ex. 20:15)? The most famous example we have of those who served God according to their own desires is Israel, and God left them! What is the purpose of the historical accounts and prophets in the Old Testament if they are not to warn us and remind us we need to follow our God? The things written before were written for our learning (see Rom. 15:4).

The church for the purpose God created is Christ's and no one else's. Think about it. If I create something, and I am not working for someone else as I create, then what I create is mine. If I buy all of the ingredients, own all of the modes of production, and do the work to build what I am making—or even if I employ people in the creation of what I am building—isn't the thing I have built mine? I have to pay the people who are helping me, and while I am paying them, they are in my employ to build what I want made. So were the apostles whom Christ our Lord sent. They served God with all of their hearts, and did so knowing they would receive a heavenly reward (see Col. 3:23–24). They served God according to the doctrine of God and not what they conjured in their minds according to their own private interpretations. As such, they have been rewarded by the King.

We all will be rewarded according to our deeds: "Eternal life to those who by patient continuance in doing good seek for glory, honor, and immortality; but to those who are self-seeking and do not obey the truth, but obey unrighteousness – indignation and wrath, tribulation and anguish, on every soul of man who does evil, of the Jew first and also of the Greek; but glory, honor, and peace to everyone who works what is good ..." (Rom. 2:7–10, 11).

Having this understanding is essential for our salvation in God. Transition this to privately owning a business. If I work hard in my business, I should reap the benefits of my work. Jesus Christ gave His life to establish a congregation, a Kingdom set apart in His name and His name only, according to His instructions. The church our Lord established is the church of Christ. Therefore, the church our Lord died for is about the business of God. Those who volunteer to serve God according to His instructions will reap the reward God wants to give to all. We just can't serve God any other way and expect to be right with God. Man has no authority to overstep this truth.

The Word of God has a lot to say about living according to selfish desires, especially when you consider that Israel desired a king to rule over them like the other nations had (see Sam. 8). If you are in a denomination or even a political organization, then you are more than likely ignoring the truth of God for a way that humans have determined to be correct. Understand that being politically correct does not make you biblically correct! Israel rejected God, desired a king and ultimately God sent Jesus. Israel crucified Jesus because they did not believe He was their King. Israel is still waiting for a physical king and that is not who the Messiah is. Read the gospel accounts for confirmation. Consider,

Jesus is a Spiritual King and not an earthly king as Israel is seeking.

Because of what man has determined to be correct, the fundamental concept of the church being Christ's is constantly under attack, and we the people are the cause. Once, only the church had lost her identity as the bride of Christ. Now we are losing all sense of identity. What was at one time obvious is no longer. Reason is being lost to desire. What God has defined is changing before our eyes. The church our Lord died for has almost become a thing of the past. We have forgotten what our Lord gave His life for.

Therefore, our man-made cultures are not our pattern for living. Our pattern for living is contained in the Word of our God. We have lost our fundamental understanding of what it means to serve according to what God has given to us, and I do not believe it is going to get better. Living as God has given is only going to become more difficult and innocent lives lost. Except for a few who would be so inclined to actually follow the Word of our Lord, "all we have gone astray; We have turned, every one, to his own way; And the Lord has laid on Him the iniquity of us all" (Isa. 53:6). This fact has not changed.

Our quest for moral autonomy has taken away our ability to understand who we are to God and our need to submit to Him. And yet God has mercy on us! Therefore, we need to change our way of thinking as we renew our minds to God and learn the true meanings of faith, love, justice, and mercy. God is the One who has shown us all of these things. I tell you we have a need to look to God for what our needs are. "For if we live in the Spirit, let us also walk in the Spirit. Let us not become conceited, provoking one another, envying one another" (Gal. 5:25–26). Let us therefore understand what is true and determine to be wise and understanding the will of the Lord (see Eph. 5:15-21).

The church is Christ's and no one else's. Christ died for His church. Denominationalism, Catholicism and Islam all steal the innocent away from God. They have determined to worship God according to their own standards instead of what our Lord has given to us.

To serve under Christ's authority is to recognize that Christ is the Head of the church. God gave our Lord this authority (see Matt. 28:18). If we desire to be right with God, we will serve according to His commandment. As the Head of the church, Christ is the owner of His body (see Eph. 5:23–32). Remember, Christ is Lord of all (see Phil. 2) and the church is His.

4

Learning about God

AFTER LIVING FOR twenty-five years without having even a little taste of who God is in my life, after struggling to live according to the dictates of men, after dreaming of being something great—I was asked one question, and I made the decision to learn about God. This was really different for me. Now I was beginning to grow.

One day I was working with a friend—who was a carpenter, of all things—and he asked me a question: "Do you know the difference between faith and belief?" Let me tell you neither of us knew about God.

After thinking for a moment and considering what the words could possibly mean, I said, "I believe you can have belief without faith, but you cannot have faith without belief. I am not certain, though, so I will ask a coworker of mine at my other job and get back with you."

Well, I asked my biblically smart coworker, and he brought me directly to the Bible. He explained that the Bible is what God has provided for us so we can know His way. It is from these words that we learn who God is and what the essential definitions of life are. In these words, which men have written according to the Holy Spirit (see 2 Pet. 1:21), we have everything we need to know about God. But just like you, how was I to know God if I was not interested or no one told me?

This was all new to me. I had not ever considered opening the Bible to look and see God. I just thought God was something else we people did or thought of and the Bible was just another book. Besides, I hated reading. The truth of the matter is I had no understanding of God or why God mattered. As I have determined, this is true of most people. What I learned after years of study is that most of us do not know God. It is not knowing or understanding who God is that keeps us from knowing how God would have us live. Makes sense, right?

I was skeptical at first as I listened to my coworker explain who God is and why we have the Bible. However, as I listened, I also began to study. Over the hours, days, weeks, months, and years, I found reason and understood I was created by God and God cared for me. As I determined to understand the difference about faith and belief I came across passages of Scripture that actually defined the two:

- Romans 6:8: "Now if we died with Christ, we believe that we shall also live with Him." This occurs through baptism. Read the rest of Romans 6. Romans 10:17: Faith comes from hearing, and hearing by the Word of God.
- 1 Corinthians 2:5: Your faith should not be in the wisdom of men but in the power of God.
- Galatians 2:20: "I have been crucified with Christ; it is no longer I who live, but Christ lives in me; and the life which I now live in the flesh, I live by faith in the Son of God, who loved me and gave Himself for me."
- Galatians 2:24: "Therefore the law was our tutor to bring us to Christ that we might be justified by faith."
- Galatians 2:25: "But after faith has come, we are no longer under a tutor."

- Galatians 2:26: "For you are all sons of God through faith in Christ Jesus."
- Ephesians 2:8: "For by grace you have been saved through faith, and that not of yourselves; it is the gift of God."
- Ephesians 4:5: "One Lord, one faith, one baptism."
- Colossians 2:12: "Buried with Him in baptism, in which you also were raised with Him through faith in the working of God, who raised Him from the dead."
- 1 Timothy 4:1: "Now the Spirit expressly says that in latter times some will depart from the faith, giving heed to deceiving spirits and doctrine of demons."
- 1 Timothy 6:12: "Fight the good fight of faith, lay hold on eternal life, to which you were also called and have confessed the good confession in the presence of many witnesses."
- 2 Timothy 4:7: "I have fought the good fight, I have finished the race, I have kept the faith."
- Hebrews 11: This chapter describes the heroes of faith.
- Hebrews 11:6: "But without faith it is impossible to please Him, for he who comes to God must believe that He is, and that He is a rewarder of those who diligently seek Him."
- James 2:17–20, 22, 24, 26: "Thus also faith by itself, if it does not have works, is dead. But someone will say, 'You have faith, and I have works.' Show me your faith without your works, and I will show you my faith by my works. You believe that there is one God. You do well. Even the demons believe – and tremble! But do you want to know, O foolish man, that faith without works is dead? ... Do you see that faith was working together with his works, and by works faith was made perfect? ... You see then that a man is justified by works, and not by faith only.... For as the body without the spirit is dead, so faith without works is dead also."

- 1 John 5:4: "For whatever is born of God overcomes the world. And this is the victory that has overcome the world – our faith."
- Jude 3: "Beloved, while I was very diligent to write to you concerning our common salvation, I found it necessary to write to you exhorting you to contend earnestly for the faith which was once for all delivered to the saints."

I learned so much when I began to read the Word of God. I began to separate myself from what I did not learn growing up. I actually began to understand life. I learned to put away the things I was accustomed to. I began to understand how God desires us to live. I began to change my ways. This is what repentance is as we are being born to the Spirit of God. My faith in God was growing and I was changing.

What really resonated with me were the Scripture passages that pointed out the division between man and man, and between man and God. There should be no division between any of us. Reading God's Word, I saw how God needs to be first in our every consideration and how we are to love one another (see Matt. 22:36-40). The wisdom of man is not what we are to trust when we look to God. In fact, we should not even look at the wisdom of men and women for how we are to live our lives unless our lives match the Word of God. God has always wanted us to trust in what He has given to us and not lean on our own understanding. We need to acknowledge Him in all our ways. He directs our paths (see Prov. 3:5).

What I learned is you cannot serve God according to the doctrine of the adversary or of men. The adversary is the same who, in the garden, tempted Eve away from God. What men and women say is the correct way to live cannot be believed when they profess another doctrine God never gave! God does not change, but we change what God has made available to us. I wish I could say differently, but men and women are not perfect, and we do have a tendency to covet. There is a bit of irony here. The fact we are not perfect is the reason we do not know God is perfect. We are perfected in Christ, though (see Heb. 10:14). So we can be perfect!

Back then, being new to the Word of God, the idea of being perfect was unconscionable to me. What could "perfect" possibly mean? As I listened to what my coworker Ralph explained to me, I needed to reason who God is in our lives and how I am to put God first in my life. I had never seen or heard from God. Why not? How did other people know who God was and I did not? Were all of these other people perfected in Christ?

After many years of study, I have learned that most people do not know God. To know God is to have a relationship with God. If we have a relationship with God, then we will learn to place God first. Placing God first is where we find the context to the purpose in our lives. Living as God lives and loving as God loves is that way. When we place God where He is first in our every consideration, life makes sense. This is because you are learning to know God.

> "Therefore do not worry, saying, "What shall we eat?" or "What shall we drink?" or "What shall we wear?" For after all these things the Gentiles seek. For your heavenly Father knows that you need all these things. But seek first the Kingdom of God and His righteousness, and all these things shall be added to you. Therefore do not worry about tomorrow, for tomorrow will worry about its own things. Sufficient for the day is its own trouble." (Matt. 6:31–34)

Since this time, I have not stopped learning about God. I have not ever stopped considering that my life is mine because God has given me this time to reconcile myself to understanding who God is to every person on this earth. There is only one God and one faith and one baptism (see Eph. 4:5). This is true no matter what others may say. Others are not inspired.

To learn about God, we must only look to what God has given to us in His Word. There we will see that what has been written has always been. This world is full of the proof we need to know God is real. We only need to seek for it. For an example, Israel is that proof we seek. We need to be understanding. We need to grow our faith and learn (see 2 Tim. 2:15).

To know God is to understand God. This is how you renew your mind to God (see Rom. 12:2).

5

How Do I Know God?

MY BELIEF IN God began with a question. My faith in God grew with the renewing of my mind to God. My obedience to God began because I desired to know how God wants His creation to be. I had reasoned the path I was on, and that path was leading me nowhere. In consideration of what I saw amongst everyone who thought they were right in their own eyes, I saw not everyone can be right according to what they desire. But who was I to question their desires. I was a person of low intelligence. I thought spending years and money learning in college was going to make me into something. I had no way of saying what was right or wrong. I guessed a lot. I just kept searching and finally a way was made known to me.

This was how I lived for the first twenty-five years of my life, trying to compete with people who came and went and held no real care for me as a person. They were just as I was. Looking to do the best they could with what they had. This I imagine is how we all are at some point in our lives. There was very little about the life I had been raised in to tell me that I needed to love my God, my neighbor, or even my brothers and sisters. I had no discipline. When I looked to Scripture, though, I found God and I found love. Ironically, my reason came to me because I desired to know God. I desired to be a part of those who had the same love for God I did. These people showed me kindness. The kinds of which I had not had growing up. I certainly was not this way!

I learned that love is much more than what we profess. Love is what God says. Consider 1 Corinthians 13:1–18. When we read what God has given to us, we can know we mean something to God and He has a plan for us. He knows us all and desires us all to know Him.

It took some years of searching after I was buried with Christ in baptism, but I finally began to see what being born of the Spirit meant. Baptism was the easy part; obedience and living as God desires was more difficult. However, I found that obeying God is not impossible. Remember John 3:5. You must have faith and know God!

Since I began my journey to a new life with God, being born of water and the Spirit, I have learned how to put together Scripture and historical facts that cannot be denied about what our God has done for us. Coming to this understanding requires time, other brethren to help, and encouragement in the knowledge of what Scripture teaches, as well as the ability to recognize what is right in front of your eyes. Obviously, this is not easy to accomplish, with all of the distractions being thrown at you by the adversary and those he is able to easily manipulate. But obedience to Christ is what we must have if we are going to live as God has said.

Two thousand years ago, a Pharisee and "a teacher of the law held in respect by all the people" acknowledged that if what Jesus was doing was of men, it would come to nothing, but if it was of God, "no one can overthrow it lest you be found to fight against God" (Acts 5:34–39). Here we are today, and Jesus is still being taught and denied continually the world over. The Pharisee was right! Jesus' coming was not of men. Today, having this understanding seems like an abstract thought about an event and a person whom most people do not spend a lot of time thinking about but say they know.

We need not look very far to put together the facts of our existence and why our Lord is important. God's Word is right in front of us, and we can know the truth of what God has given to us. Unfortunately, most people simply do not care what we have before us. They, and possibly you, are always looking for something more to justify their existence or take up their time. We cling to what others create and to our own thoughts, never considering that we have God right in front of us and how important that is.

I am saddened to see even most of our elderly are immature in the faith God wants us all to have. They should know better. Instead, what is ingrained within their being is the tradition of their individual lives. They have been indoctrinated by the desires and commandments of men over the commandments of God. As Jesus said "in vain they worship Me, teaching as doctrines the commandments of men." (Matt. 15:9).

We should not be this way, but unfortunately, this is the way we grow. We grow within the context of our individual cultures and thoughts instead of the context of God. As we grow, we fail to do root-cause analysis. We do not know the context of our lives. If we would just look to what God has given to us, we would be looking into things that are of a Spiritual nature. But we simply cannot understand what we do not see. Ever since the garden of Eden, we have pushed God out of our sight. Now it is no wonder we cannot see God.

The way God wants us to live is clearly articulated through the Word He has given to us. You can understand this if you are willing to devote yourself to living as God has designed. This is how you are renewed in the "Spirit of your mind" (Eph. 4:23). We are to walk differently (Eph. 4.17-23). Remember this.

We are without excuse if we say we do not know or cannot know who God is and what He expects from us. The truth of God is right in front of us, yet we can think of every reason to not look at what God has prepared for us. The way we are to live is not within ourselves, but from our God. Isn't this what is written from our Lord Jesus Christ in Matthew 6:33? What about in the prophets of God? The world has been told, warned, encouraged to seek God for thousands of year and yet we remain far from God.

Since the beginning of time, God has been leading us and we have been leaving Him. It is the adversary who placed a wedge between God and our thoughts. This has resulted in our actions separating us from our God (see Isa. 59:2). We do not even care to understand this fact. Most people are convinced in their own minds that they are living correctly, and this is not true. Sadly, people who believe this are lost. They are hypocrites, just as Isaiah described. Jesus explained, "These people draw near to Me with their mouth, and honor Me with their lips, But their heart is far from Me" (Matt. 15:8).

We believe by the things we do that we are justified. Who is it that justifies? It is God (see Rom. 8:33). Therefore, we must be renewed in the spirit of our minds to have any hope of justification before God.

We have lost sight of our God because of any excuse you can think of. But we are able to read what God has left for us in the Word He has given to us. We can see what our actions have done and the results of ignoring and leaving our Lord. When we ignore God, we not only deprive ourselves, but we deprive future generations of the faith we all should have in God. Yes, each generation is guilty of this negligence, and the truth of what God has given to us drifts further and further away. Unbelief in God creates an unsafe space for everyone.

As I have come to the understanding of who God is, I have tried to wrap my head around why I need to believe what we have in God's Word. I have done a lot of study and I have done a lot of thinking as I reconcile what God has given to us with how the world is acting. I have put together what is written in the Word of God with what our actual history tells us, and I cannot justify not believing in our God. This is faith! For me not to believe in

God and His Son Jesus Christ would be the same as saying I do not believe what I see right before my eyes. It would be the same as ignoring the facts of our existence, and I cannot do this.

The evidence (Israel) is overwhelming concerning who we are and where we have come from. At least for now anyway. The fact we disbelieve in God means we have usurped what we have always had before us. Thank God for His patient endurance of us. We still have time to come to the acknowledgment that what has been written was written for our learning. Through what has been written, we are to patiently come to understand that God is (see 2 Tim. 3:16–17). If we choose not to study as we have been commanded, we will never learn what God has given to us (see 2 Tim. 2:15). Then we will be without excuse when we are judged by God on the last day (see John 12:48–50).

God exists. The record of our existence explains this fact. Ever since creation, for us to believe in God, we must have faith. Remember the question my friend asked me? What is the difference between faith and belief?

For faith in God to grow, you must be willing to set aside all of the distractions of the world and give God the attention He deserves. Getting the context of our lives correct depends upon our coming to God as He has said and growing within this context. We need to come to God on the terms He has given to us. Those terms are written and have been preserved for us. They are available in every language on earth. If we choose not to study God's Word, we ignore what God has put right in front of our eyes. Now, we are without excuse (see Rom. 1:20).

Scripture is everywhere. It is thousands of years old. There are people in existence today whose history is explained both in God's Word and in our secular history, through books and artifacts. These tells us we should be looking to God so that we can know who God is. But we choose not to because we refuse to place 2+2 together and God remains far from us. The pride of life and the need to exist according to what has become the man-made standard has kept us from living as our God desires us to. We have put ourselves in the place of God. The evidence of God is right in front of us, but most of us will not believe. We do not understand the circumstances that form the setting of our lives. Genesis 1–5 explains the perfection we were given and the perfection we rejected.

Most of the world's population says they do not believe in God, and this is evidenced by their deeds. I believe our unbelief is mostly due to willful ignorance and a continued negligence about what God has instructed us to do. People ignore God for what the world has to offer. Negligence breeds ignorance and contempt. This is a vicious cycle. We do not love that which we do not know or understand. You may say you love, but actions speak loudly.

God wants us to know Him, and Jesus explained this fact all too well. We need to actively pursue the things of God in order to grow in our understanding of God. If you pursue the pleasures of this world, things that do not endear you to God, you will fall short of what God wants to give to you. You will fall in line with the position of the adversary.

Remember, God wants to be first in our lives (see Matt. 6:33). God wants to give you a place in His Kingdom, the Paradise of God. God wants you to love Him and your neighbor. God loves us! God is the final Lawgiver and Judge. We must live with this commonsense understanding that God is our Creator or be forever suffering wrong. We cannot walk outside of what God has given to us and expect to think God is okay with us doing so.

As you think about the way our world is today, you can see we live in confusion about who our God is. Some are even confused about their gender. How is this? This confusion is exactly what was desired by the serpent in the garden of Eden. We have the story of our creation before us, and we can understand it. God made one environment for humans to exist in, and God was right there among the people. When confronted with something different from what God had said, we had a choice to make. We chose wrong. This was our beginning, but it does not need to be our ending. Today, just as yesterday, God has given us a way out. Jesus came and died to give us the opportunity to change our lives. We can die to sin to live in the Spirit. This is our choice.

However, because of the adversarial serpent in the garden of Eden and his desire to change our devotion to what is right, we are now separated from God. The adversary of God took us away from God because we were too weak in our minds to stand firm on what God had given to us. Thus, we were unable to remain in God's presence. This is why we need to keep God in front of us at all times and write His Word on our hearts (Deut. 11:18–19). It takes work to live as God desires us to live. We must work at learning about God so we can know Him!

So it is that Adam and Eve—and we—chose to do as we desired and not what God had said. We did not keep God first. We were lulled into believing a lie. Today, we have very little understanding that what happened before was the cause of all our confusion concerning the one God we have always had before us. Six thousand years after Adam and Eve, we are continually fumbling over ourselves to decide what is right and wrong. Sad.

Some learned people, doctors of psychology and atheists particularly, like to call what God has given to us a myth. They add to the confusion about what our existence keeps demonstrating is true. They question the faith Christians have in preference for what they call logical thought. But how do they know that what they think is logical? Who told them it was logical? Did God tell them or a secular college professor? Did they rationalize this of their own will?

Our Bible, the Word of our God, is very clear about our existence. Our history proves the Bible is true. The only way people will understand our existence is to reconcile what has been with what actually is. We must remember we are not right in our own eyes concerning who God is. God has told us who He is. Read your Bible and grow your faith in God.

6

The Construct of God's Word

THE FACT THAT we have God's Word available to us almost everywhere and in any language should be well-known. Because we have what is written, we can know the Spirit God desires us to attain. To this purpose, the Bible is the most-translated and most-copied book of all time. Here are some examples of Scriptures which describe how we are to be in the Spirit: Matt. 11:28, Matt. 20:25-28, Luke 22:27-30, John 13:12-17. The Scriptures are clear about our need to renew our minds to the Spirit of God (see Rom. 12:2). They are written for our learning (see Rom. 15:4). Indeed the greatest purpose we can have is to learn how to serve. Our Lord is coming to reward us according to our work (see Rev. 22:12). We need to be ready.

The Bible tells us the story of all creation, who we are to God, that we disobeyed God, and how we can get back to God. Outside of Christianity, there are many different religions that do not have the evidence of what God has purposed as the Bible does. Though other religions say they are true, don't be deceived by the false teachings of men and women. We have historical evidence pointing to what the Scriptures tell us and even living examples of a people whose beginnings are recorded in God's Word (the Israelites and Arabs, etc.). As your honest study bears this out, be discerning and understanding. Seek for the truth of God. We have the truth of God, and we can know it. Remember, "faith comes by hearing, and hearing by the word of God" (Romans 10:17). Study to learn (see 2 Tim. 2:15).

The Bible is written in sections that describe various points in time from the creation up to approximately the end of the first century CE. The book of Genesis gets us started on our historical journey. Here, we see creation and we see God's provision for us. In the very first verse of the Bible, we are introduced to God as Elohim. This word is actually *'elohiym* and is the plural of *'elowahh* (discussed previously). They are God our Creator; a very important fact in our understanding.

Adam and Eve are introduced methodically in chapters 1 through 3. We are also introduced to a subversive character called the adversary, represented by a serpent in the garden of Eden in Genesis 3. As I have already pointed out, the serpent is the reason for our chaos today. The adversary set us in conflict with our God when he tempted Eve and suggested God was lying to her. The adversary is the reason we doubt God. This fact is very important.

It was this adversary who led us to be tempted. Specifically, Adam and Eve were tempted. Temptation led us into sin, which is what separates us from God. We did wrong. But it gets worse. In Genesis chapters 4 and 6, we are introduced to jealousy, murder and the destruction of the earth by a flood because of humanity's continued sin. Our God had enough of the debauchery humanity enjoyed living in, and God destroyed the world. Just like today, people living at the time of the Flood refused to look to God, but instead fell headlong into godless desires.

Even so, within these chapters we can also see a promise God made to us so we could know for certain that the earth will never be destroyed by a flood again—the rainbow. God made the rainbow as a promise of His mercy toward us. The rainbow is a sign from God (see Gen. 9:13). The rainbow is not a sign of homosexual pride, though people would like to say otherwise. Remember debauchery? Homosexuality is one of the reasons the earth was destroyed. Our continued sin is the reason we do not have God in our midst any longer. Sexual proclivity and love are mutually exclusive. Remember there are different types of love in the world that the Bible describes.[3] God's reason needs to come before our desire.

Today for us to know God, it is up to us to read what God has given to us through the Word we have as written (see John 1:1-5). Through the Word of God, we can know God and how to come back to God. Not looking to God's Word to find God is not wise and a reason we do not understand who God is to us. Just as before, we have made our gods.

Beginning with the book of Genesis, we get quite a bit of insight into who our God is and what He has done for us. Likewise, we can see what we have done to Him and to each other. Because of the book of Genesis, specifically chapters 1 through 3, we should know how our relationship with God needs to be. We should have faith in God and be sinless! We need to acknowledge God in all our ways (see Pro. 3). We should not ignore the Word of God. Instead, we should embrace what is written and learn the perfection of what God has given to us. We are in harmony with God when we follow God. But we sinned, and from sin came more sin, until the only remedy God sought was to destroy what He had created. You see, even if you do things within the integrity of your heart, this does not make you right in the sight of God. See the example of Abimelech in Genesis 20.6. Even today if you refuse to do what is right, God will give you over to your unclean heart filled lust (see Rom. 1:24). This is why we teach. Yet still, people would rather be condemned because of their love for pleasure instead of their love for God (see 2 Thes. 2:11-12).

---

[3] Strong, James; Vine, W.E., *The New Strong's Concise Concordance* & Vines Concise Dictionary of the Bible (Nashville: Thomas Nelson, 1997, 1999), 225.

Bill Mitchell

In the book of Genesis, we see that Noah and his family were saved from sin and debauchery by water when God flooded the earth. Noah was found to be right with God and everyone else was not (see Gen. 6). Noah did as our God instructed and was saved as the wicked were swept away in the flood. Remember, the wicked mocked Noah, but Noah was faithful. We know this example is a precursor to our being dead to sin through baptism. This fact is ignored by much of what the world calls Christianity thanks to denominational preachers and other false teachers.

But look at 1 Peter 3:18-22:

> "For Christ also suffered once for sins, the just for the unjust, that He might bring us to God, being put to death in the flesh but made alive by the Spirit, by whom also He went and preached to the spirits in prison, who formerly were disobedient, when once the Divine longsuffering waited in the days of Noah, while *the* ark was being prepared, in which a few, that is, eight souls, were saved through water. There is also an antitype which now saves us—baptism (not the removal of the filth of the flesh, but the answer of a good conscience toward God), through the resurrection of Jesus Christ, who has gone into heaven and is at the right hand of God, angels and authorities and powers having been made subject to Him."

One does not need to look very far to understand the truth. The truth is everywhere. I know the truth by faith because I trust what has been written. The first letter of Peter in 3:18–22 tells us just how important we are to God, and that it is water which cleanses us. We only need to come to it. Water is what Christ commanded us to be born of to die to sin; "For he who has died

48

has been freed from sin" (Rom. 6:1-7). Sin will be all around us regardless, but because we desire to be different and be with God, we will renew our minds to God. We will be walking as God has given us the ability (see Rom. 12:2). Since the Scriptures have been written everyone can reconcile their lives to God when we read what the truth says and apply the truth to our lives (see Jas. 2:17). When we do as our Lord commands, we are doing right by God. If what some person says contradicts what is written, then we need to look to the source for correction. We cannot just say "this is my faith" and expect to be living correctly as God has instructed. Your trust must be based in what God has instructed. We will see this example in Sarah below. What God has given to us is "thoroughly equipped for every good work" (2 Tim. 3:17). To this purpose we shall learn our need to live as God has given and not as we believe in our hearts without any knowledge of who our God is.

In God's Word, the first five books of the Bible are called the Torah in Hebrew, also known as the Five Books of Moses. The Torah comprises Genesis, Exodus, Leviticus, Numbers, and Deuteronomy. The Torah was written by the prophet Moses, who was a forerunner of our Lord. The Torah was written between approximately 1500 and 1400 BCE, or before our Lord. As I understand, this is about the time when the Hebrews began writing.

As Israel was making their trek to the Land of Promise when they left Egypt, Moses received the Ten Commandments from God upon Mount Sinai. We see this in the book of the Exodus, which describes how Moses and Aaron led the Israelites from Egypt. What Moses wrote was how Israel developed into a nation of God (consider Spiritual and physical attributes) that began with a promise God gave to Abraham. Moses also told Israel that if they were not obedient to our God, then they would not inherit the Land of Promise. Read Deuteronomy for confirmation. This is exactly where Israel is today. The land Israel occupies today is not theirs according to the promise of God. Instead, it exists due to man-made legal decree.

There is a lot of detail behind what I am telling you in brief. I encourage you to read your Bible, because naturally the Bible does a great job with this explanation. We can trust it. I believe what is written to be true, because I believe in God. Just as Israel was given the opportunity to live with God, we are as well, but only if we have trusting faith in God. This is no different than what Israel needed to have.

For example, in the book of Genesis, God chose a man named Abraham to be the recipient of three promises. Who was Abraham? Abraham was called by God and is the father of Ishmael, Isaac and Jacob (Israel) through Isaac (the lineage of promise). Abraham is the father of Ishmael not according to the promise of God but born of the bondwoman, Hagar, who was the servant of Abraham's wife Sarah. Though Abraham and Sarah had the promise of God, Sarah gave Hagar, her servant to Abraham to bear a son for her, Ishmael. Perhaps Sarah was presumptuous or unbelieving? What I do know about Sarah is that she desired a child. By faith, I also know the promise of God does not fail.

On a personal note, though I know this, I still fall short.

Before Jacob (Israel) was born, Abraham was the father of Isaac, the son of the promise God made to Abraham and Sarah (see Gen. 15-18:15). God kept His promise to Abraham and Sarah even though their faith waned. Their faith (like ours) was lacking. Their untrusting faith resulted in what has become the nation of Islam. But through Isaac, Abraham would be given a land that would be where the great nation of God would dwell, and in him all the families of the earth would be blessed (see Gen. 12:1–3). This construct helps us to see our need to trust only in God.

Let's take a closer look at who Abraham was, because Abraham is central to our understanding of the faith we are to have in God.

Abraham was descended from Adam and Eve through Seth, Methuselah, Lamech, Noah, Shem, and Terah, among others (see Luke 3:34–38). Abraham is important for us to know because his example of faith in God shows us how the promises of God have been fulfilled. But even with Abraham's great faith, he was not a man of perfect faith.

Still, it is written that Abraham was a man of faith (see Heb. 11:8-12). This is how we are to be. Abraham believed in God, and God called Abraham into service. Abraham believed and obeyed God, and Abraham was called righteous (see Gen. 12–25). Abraham was obedient to God, and therefore, God made promises to Abraham. Today, we are the recipients of these promises through Jesus Christ, our Messiah and Savior who came from the lineage of Isaac. As you should understand according to the Scriptures, Ishmael had no part in our salvation from God.

Jesus was a man of perfect faith. God's plan was always for us to live with Him, but at the appointed time, there was only one person who ever lived whom God saw as the One who could fulfill what He desired for all of humankind. Jesus is that person, God in the flesh (see Matt. 1:23). The One sent from God for our redemption (see Gal. 4:1-4:5). What this just shows us is how great the grace of God is! Ever since our falling away in the garden, our unbelief has emboldened us for our purposes and not what God purposed for us. We need to trust in God just as Abraham.

God used Abraham because of Abraham's faithfulness. Abraham was told by God to move from his homeland to a land known as Canaan, or what is present-day Israel. There, Abraham was given two sons in his old age and there he was buried near Hebron in the cave of Machpelah (see Gen. 17-25:7–10).

As I have mentioned, Abraham also had another son, not according to the promise. Let's see what the desire of Sarah caused. Abraham and Sarah's first son's name was Ishmael, whom scholars say is the progenitor of the Arabs, both messenger and prophet.[4] This lineage is important to the third Abrahamic religion called Islam. (The first two being Judaism and Christianity). Although Ishmael is not the son of promise as Isaac was, the angel of God still said to his mother, Hagar that he would be a great nation (see Gen. 21:18). Even still, since the years of 609 – 632 AD, that is, after Christ—Mohammad is said to have received revelations from the archangel Gabriel to institute the religion of Islam[5]. Again, just as denominational preachers teach error of what Scripture actually says, here we have a "prophet" teaching error many centuries after Scripture had already "once been delivered to the Saints" (Jude 3). Certainly the angel Gabriel would not lie (see Luke 1:19). Perhaps the coming of Islam is just an example of the strong delusion God has given. The claim that Islam is where salvation comes is against what God has revealed through His Son Jesus Christ and is an error much of the world is swept away in. This error has caused many problems just as all of what man conjures in his mind about God causes. Remember, God will send strong delusion upon those who would believe the lie (see 2 Thes. 2:9–12).

Therefore, according to the Scriptures of God and His promise, Abraham fathered Isaac through Sarah, and Isaac fathered Jacob, who would become Israel. From Jacob would come twelve tribes who would form the nation of Israel (Jacob). This fact cannot be denied. We can see it every day and have verifiable living proof of this truth. The biblical record verifies what we see! We know the nation of Israel did not necessarily trust in God and they were caused to wonder. But to fulfill God's promises, God gave the land of Canaan to Israel just as recorded in the book of Joshua.

Israel would become a great nation. But so too is Ishmael. However, the nation of Israel is the nation God chose to be His

---

[4] https://www.britannica.com/biography/Ishmael-son-of-Abraham
[5] https://en.wikipedia.org/wiki/Quran

people. From Abraham through Isaac and Jacob would come Moses of the tribe of Levi, who would lead the people to the Promised Land, though he would not enter in. This is the story of the Exodus from Egypt, which is further described in the books of Leviticus, Numbers, and Deuteronomy.

Moses did not enter into the Land of Promise because he did not observe the commandment of God (see Deut. 32:49-51). Instead, Joshua, the student of Moses, led the people across the Jordan. There the tribes of Israel inherited the land according to the promise of God and there Israel ultimately lost this land due to their unwillingness to do as God said. The story of this loss encompasses most of the books of the Old Testament. It could be said Israel did not understand the spiritual nature of their obedience to God. How about us? Remember, we are to be born of water and the Spirit to enter the Kingdom of God!

Keep in mind the fact of Israel losing the Promised Land for their lack of obedience to God as you read the Bible. Israel thought they were doing what God wanted them to, but God had left them because they were not. Israel expected and still expects an earthly king. But this is wrong. God sent His Son as a sacrifice for their sin and ultimately for all people (Read the Gospels and Acts). Israel had their chance to be our example for good, but they lost this chance due to their sin. They did not have faith in God. Consider the claim of Mohammed even after 500 plus years that the Christ came to bring salvation to all men (see Tit. 2:11). Error abounds and whole nations are lost.

Today, as in the day of our Lord, we need to be obedient through faith in Christ and do as He commands to come back to God. Just like Israel and Islam, we cannot come to God on our own terms and expect God to accept this. God is clear. We must understand what is written for us to come back to God. As I have said previously, we can lose our salvation!

Let's look at an ever-so-brief summary of the books and periods in the Bible.

1. *Genesis*: Our creation, our falling away from God, and God's love for us is shown.

2. *Exodus, Leviticus, Numbers, and Deuteronomy*: Israel is led to the Land of Promise by Moses, following God's instructions. They are given rules and regulations to help them see what sin is and their necessity to live as God has said.

3. *Joshua*: This book describes the conquest of the Land of Promise.

4. *Judges – Ruth*: Israel falls away from God, forgetting entirely what God has given them according to His Spirit and desiring a king to lead them instead. Ruth shows us a glimmer of hope. Again, God shows His mercy to Israel while also giving them over to their evil desires. This leads to their weakening as a nation. Keep this in mind!

5. *I Samuel through 2 Chronicles*: These books present historical background regarding Israel's kings and their continued captivity for not following God. This is what sin causes. Consider the turmoil still going on in the Middle East today. This turmoil has never stopped.

6. *Ezra through Songs*: These books describe Israel's return from captivity and their wisdom literature.

7. *Isaiah through Malachi*: The prophets of God are sent to Israel after the conquest of the Promised Land that Israel might repent and turn back to God.

8. *Intertestamental period*: This is an era of approximately four hundred years of silence when God did not communicate with Israel as in times before.

   • Israel made their own laws, which today are still used religiously. This is manifest in what is known as Halachah (Jewish Law) adjudicated through the Bet Din (rabbinical court). Nothing to do with God, but instead man made legal decree.

- Israel believes they are right in their own eyes, just as most of us do. This is wrong today just as it was before (see Judg. 17:6). God remains Supreme and Israel rejects our Lord. Don't be like Israel. Do not justify your sin.

9. *Matthew, Mark, Luke and John*: The gospel books describe the history of the Messiah, our Lord and Savior, Jesus Christ, who was spoken of by the prophets in the Old Testament.

   - Jesus Christ is the King given to Israel, but Israel rejected Him because Jesus was not a man according to their expectations. Israel, like most of us today, make Jesus, our God in the flesh, who we desire Him to be instead of submitting ourselves to what He has said. Consider Matthew 21.

10. *Acts*: This book describes the beginning of the church of our Lord, who is King forevermore—hence the Kingdom of God.

11. *Romans through Jude*: These books contain letters to Christians in various places who are being taught according to the truth of God.

12. *Revelation*: The last book of the Bible describes what our Lord revealed to John, His apostle. Here we find out many things, but importantly, we discover what not to do. This so we can get back to the Paradise of God (see Rev. 2:7).

7

A Few More Things You Should Know

NOW, IT SHOULD go without saying we need to get back to learning the Word of God. Remember, we need to know God. We need to understand why we have gone so far away from God and as I have been pointing out, we need to understand what it means to live as God would have us live, in the Spirit of God. Again, read what Jesus says in John 3:5. We need to live as God has said, regardless of what we believe or claim our faith to be. If you are struggling in life, then turn to God as your resource for living. As you have read thus far and seen examples of, your personal belief is not going to save you unless it is based in what God has given to us.

Early in the history of humankind, people knew God face-to-face. People knew God through angels and prophets. Only a few lived according to what God gave to us. Today we need to read the Word of God, the Bible, so we can understand where to place our trust. We need to understand that "it is better to trust in the Lord than to put confidence in man" (Ps. 118:8). But how do we do this when men and women have become as "those who desire an opportunity to be regarded just as we are in the thing of which they boast. For such are false apostles, deceitful workers, transforming themselves into apostles of Christ. And no wonder! For Satan himself transforms into an angel of light. Therefore it is no great thing if his ministers also transform themselves into ministers of righteousness, whose end will be according to their works" (2 Cor. 11:12–15). More teachers than not seem to be this way. They desire to be leaders to God, but do not have our God within them. (see Thes. 2:9-12).

Today, we exist far away from the understanding of God. For us to understand the words of God, we need to know why the Word of God was given to us and how we fit into its context. Essentially, we need to grow our faith in God because without faith, we have nothing. We simply search day-to-day, thinking the only purpose we have in life is our pleasure and work, and this at almost any cost. We need to live by faith in God, according to the gospel, because this is how the righteous are to live (see Rom. 1:16–17). Instead, God is ignored. Families and brethren are constantly separated due to a selfish and self defeating mindset.

> "*There is* therefore now no condemnation to those who are in Christ Jesus, who do not walk according to the flesh, but according to the Spirit. For the law of the Spirit of life in Christ Jesus has made me free from the law of sin and death. For what the law could not do in that it was weak through the flesh, God *did* by sending His own Son in the likeness of sinful flesh, on account of sin: He condemned sin in the flesh, that the righteous requirement of the law might be fulfilled in us who do not walk according to the flesh but according to the Spirit. For those who live according to the flesh set their minds on the things of the flesh, but those *who live* according to the Spirit, the things of the Spirit. For to be carnally minded *is* death, but to be spiritually minded *is* life and peace. Because the carnal mind *is* enmity against God; for it is not subject to the law of God, nor

indeed can be. So then, those who are in the flesh cannot please God" (Rom. 8:1-8).

When we refuse to enjoin ourselves in the work that God would have us to do, spiritually speaking, we are of little good to anyone except ourselves. We see how this has gone. History is full of these examples. Because of this manner of living, we need to know and recognize how our God has made us. We are to be as people who serve in Spirit and in Truth (see John 4:24).

Here are some basics of what you should know about the content of God's Word:

More on Construct: God has always given us His Word to live by. God has never left us empty-handed. We are the ones who have gone away from God and said we do not want or need God. We have made our gods. God has always instructed us in right living so we could stay in His presence, but we have largely ignored this for what has become our self-righteousness. We ignore God because we do not believe what He has given us is true. But thank God for His great love for us! (see 1 John 3:24). Today just as yesterday, we mostly do not know this fact as we have collectively forgotten about God. As the created of God, we have rejected Him, just as an unbelieving child rejects their parents.

God in times before spoke to us person to person, as in the garden of Eden with Adam and Eve. God even spoke to Cain before and after he killed his brother. God also spoke to people through angels and prophets, the last prophet being our Lord and Savior, Jesus Christ. We the people have dropped the ball in teaching ourselves about God and conveying what we need to know about God to others, especially our children. This should not be so. Instead, we have let our "cultures" dictate who we are to God and this is not correct. What we need to know about our salvation, God has made available to us through Jesus Christ. Most just refuse to believe and the framework is gone. God's grace means nothing to these people. Thank God for His mercy because we still have time to repent and obey.

Age: The age of the Bible is quite old, but not as many years old as God's communication with man. The Word of God is not even the oldest writing we have. God's communication with us has been happening since the beginning of time though. The Bible is roughly 3,500 years old, counting the Old Testament and the New Testament. The New Testament was written in the first century CE, just 1,900 years ago. As the ages have gone on, God has given us over to ourselves. This is because mankind has ignored God and not reconciled their lives to God. Just as children get older and desire their own way, we desired the same from God—not because this is right, but it is because this is what we desire. Generally, just as a parent will not hold back a child whose desire is to come out from parental protection, God has let us do the same. Age does not make us smarter; it only makes us older. Experience through learning makes us smarter. Discipline in love is not a bad thing—except to those who refuse to listen. These people abound causing great errors to be made.

Books: There are sixty-six books in the Bible, authored by many different people. There are believed to be thirty-two authors of the Old Testament books and nine authors of the New Testament books. The Bible was put together over the span of approximately fifteen hundred years, from BCE 1400 to 90 CE. I am not going to be dogmatic about the age of the Canon of God, because what is important is why we have what is written. The time is accurate, though, according to scholars. Look it up.

Falling Away: Falling away is a result of not believing in our Lord and our God. This is what sin causes: it keeps us away from God. Why would we believe in God when we do not care to? God needs to be first in our lives, but we do not know this. For most, the thought of our God never enters the mind. Sin takes over, and people never know any differently, trusting in their own ways of living. In this, God is taken out of the picture. We fail to see just how vital the knowledge of who God is and what God has done for us is to our lives. We believe more in the moments we are in, not understanding God has given us all things that we need to live with Him. I will say again, most never understand what it means to be born of water and the Spirit. We continue our unbelief in God. What most people believe is that "God so loved the world that He gave His only begotten Son, that whoever believes in Him should not perish but have everlasting life" (John 3:16). They ignore the rest of what John said. Do not be fooled. Study. John 3:5 is clear.

Sin: Sin is what separates us from God. Sin is the result of falling away. Sin is missing the mark (see Heb. 4:1). Look to Genesis 1, through the story of Noah, for more detail about how sin separates us from God. You will see where we were with God and where we desired to go after we left God. God was still there for us, but we needed to look to God for our sustenance. Most of the protagonists of the Old Testament have clearly shown they did not do this. Only some of the leaders whom God gave the opportunity to serve Him did what God desired.

The Bible contains important books that help us understand how God deals with us and our selfish desires. Through it all, God continues to be merciful. We, however, continue in sin, thinking grace will continue to abound as we live our lives as selfishly as we desire and with a lack of accountability. Know this: "The wages of sin is death, but the gift of God is eternal life in Christ Jesus our Lord" (Rom. 6:23). God is watching. If only people paid attention, they would have the ability to know. Life could be better especially considering the present circumstances where many people justify themselves by themselves. This is wrong.

Salvation: Salvation is the remedy to heal us and bring us back to God. Jesus Christ is the way. Jesus said, "I am the way, the truth, and the life. No one comes to the Father except through Me" (John 14:6). Jesus instructed His apostles, and the apostles instructed their disciples in the way of our Lord (see Matt.

28:18-20). His story has not gone away. Our salvation comes from faithful obedience and dying to sin (see John 3:5). Jesus's death on the cross did not automatically wipe our sin away. Be understanding. We need to do more than just believe. We need to act! Jesus's death on the cross made it possible for us to come in contact with His blood. Read every account of how people were saved in the book of Acts for confirmation. Please read Romans 6, Galatians 3:27, and the last words written of Jesus in Matthew 28. This will get you on the right path of understanding how important it is that we die to sin and renew our minds to God (again, see Rom. 12:2). God has always wanted us to be with Him, but it is our sin that separates us from our God. Without being born of water and the Spirit, we cannot enter the kingdom of God. There is simply no salvation in any other than Jesus Christ (see Acts 4:12).

> "I have been crucified with Christ; it is no longer I who live, but Christ lives in me; and the *life* which I now live in the flesh I live by faith in the Son of God, who loved me and gave Himself for me" (Gal. 2:20).

8

Read Your Bible and Study to Show Yourself Approved of God

BY NOW, WE should all know God and that our sin is what separates us from God. Our sin is the reason humanity was removed from the garden of Eden, the Paradise of God—the Kingdom of God. We live outside of what God purposed for us because of our sin and there is no way to get back to God unless our sin is taken out of the way.

Sin (*hamartia*) means to miss the mark.[6] Sin is going against God and the reason God sent His Son (see John 1:29). Today we justify all we are and do because we refuse to acknowledge this fundamental fact God has given to us. We can know right and wrong, but most choose to do wrong never understanding we are to know God and obey Him (see Luke 9:35). The truth is we have a collective inability to give God the glory He deserves. God gave us free will, but He also gave us instructions about how we are to live our lives. Today those instructions are found in the Bible. Back in the garden, it was God, Adam and Eve, and the adversary of God. Today, we still have God, but we ignore God

---

[6] Strong, James; Vine, W.E., *The New Strong's Concise Concordance* & Vines Concise Dictionary of the Bible (Nashville: Thomas Nelson, 1997, 1999), 345.

because we believe we have all the answers. Ironically, those who say they have the answers refuse to acknowledge God. They do not realize this is an adversarial position.

Remember Genesis 3? We do not realize God gave us over to our desire which necessitated we leave His presence. When Adam and Eve took heed to the adversary, they broke faith with God. Today, as you can imagine most people do not believe in God. Life has become that faith is almost impossible to come by. Rather, most believe in the manifestations of their intent, believing only in what they see and hold. In the end, this is no help unless our intent is to be reconciled to God. Sadly, based on what I see every day, I do not believe mankind desires reconciliation to God.

Understand, what I have written is not to take the place of what God has given to us in His Word. What I have written will, I hope, help you to see your importance to God, and to see the need we have to come back to God as we acknowledge Him in all our ways (see Prov. 3:6). Think of what I have written as a sermon. Listen when I say that not knowing or caring about God is the largest problem we face today. It is the largest problem because of the mass confusion we live in and need to live through. I assert that we do not know how we fit in contextually with God and most seek self justification. This is because of our continued disobedience to God and disrespect for one another. We need to understand the way of God, love God and one another. This means living in accord with what has been written for our learning (see Rom. 15:4).

Who is it that understands Jesus gave us two basic commandments?

> "Then one of them, a lawyer, asked Him a question, testing Him, and saying, "'Teacher, which is the great commandment in the law?'" Jesus said to him, "'You shall love the Lord your God with all your heart, with all your soul, and

with all your mind." This is the first and great commandment. And the second is like it: "You shall love your neighbor as yourself." On these two commandments hang all the Law and the Prophets.'" (Matt. 22:35–40)

But we believe we are the product of many different thoughts and ways, and that we do not have any need to submit ourselves to God. This is true to a point. However, our points need their foundation upon God's eternal Word, which tells us where we fit in. No matter how great we believe we are, God is greater. Naturally, then, it is essential we understand how to place God in our lives. God needs to be first in our every consideration for us to be right with God. This begins, today as every day, with reading His Word. When we know God, we are living right!

But even with the Word of God before us since the beginning of time, whether spoken or written, we do not respect God as we need to. We do not know just how important we are to God. There is a void in our lives, and that void is where our God should be! I believe this is due to the fact we have become autonomous moral agents of our own making. This is not true. We are not autonomous moral agents. God just gave us over to ourselves because of our disobedience (see Rom. 1.24) and sadly most never understand how to fill this void.

Because of this, we have very little to no faith in God. Generation after generation refuses to live as God has given, or to teach their children and others about God. This way of living is wrong and a product of what the adversary has placed into our minds. The adversary desires to separate us from God (see Gen. 3).

Do not get me wrong. We willingly gave our thoughts over to not believing in God because of our desires and because we did not love the truth (see 2 Thess. 2:9–11). Past this explanation, I am trying to speak to our need for reconciliation to God. Every day is the time we need to search for God. He is not far from us (see Acts 17). God is always ready for us to submit ourselves to Him. In fact, God is patiently waiting for us to reconcile ourselves to Him. The great day of the Lord will come, when all will be held accountable (see Acts 2; Joel 2:31). We need to be ready!

Life is much easier when we rely on our God according to His Word. Life makes a lot more sense and tensions are lifted as we rely on what God has given to us. As we congregate in an assembly of those who are like-minded. Unfortunately, there will always be people who desire to break the bond you are trying to create as you bring the context of your life back to God. So be strong in the faith because we are not perfect.

There are many "good" people in the world who do not know God, who do not believe in God nor trust in Him, and who only consider what they believe in as their god(s). These people need to learn the truth of our God and our lives in Him. We need to submit ourselves to God and let go of the worldliness that encompasses us. Remember that, because of the adversary, we are the ones who created worldliness instead of listening to God. The adversary trapped us to take us out of the protection God gave to us! God has always been for us even when collectively we refuse to acknowledge Him. We need to understand God created the rules of life. Rules are color blind, sadly, people are not.

It is an amazing concept for us to grasp that we can still get authority from God to live as He desires us to live with Him in His Kingdom. Being with our Lord is that way. God is just waiting for us, and we need to know this. This is why I am writing and teaching. I want to help you see your need to put God first in all you do and learn to trust our Almighty Creator and not yourself. But for this, you must believe in God. That having been said, there are only two basic commandments we need to know, as I have already pointed out: to love the Lord our God with all our hearts, with all our souls, and with all our minds; and to love our neighbor as ourselves (see Matt. 22:35–40). Remember, it is for these two commandments from God based in love that our Lord was killed.

People (Israel and the Romans, by way of biblical example) were simply unwilling to submit themselves to what our Lord taught about the Kingdom of God. Today, nothing has really changed. Most people would rather rely on their self justification or traditions. This is why there is so much division. We have very little unity because of what people create. As I have already said, not obeying God is missing the mark. It means living in eternal damnation, away from the Paradise of God (John 5:29). This we should not do because we are not our own. Jesus bought us (see 1 Cor. 6:20). Jesus became sin for us, that we might become the righteousness of God in Him (see 2 Cor. 5:21). To live for our Lord is how we have the unity of the Spirit and the bond of peace (see Eph. 4:3).

Unfortunately, most people do not know what this means because they do not study to know God. They do not study because they do not care to know God. Instead, we search for the things of life that confound our understanding of God. Most do not even comprehend our need to renew our minds to God to know His will (see Rom. 12:2).

9

This World Is Not Our Home

READING GOD'S WORD, I learned, "Your faith should not be in the wisdom of men but in the power of God" (1 Cor. 2:5).

When I read Scripture for the first time, I began to learn about God. I saw I could not reason the things of God on my own. I had His story right in front of me. Coming to this understanding required me to have faith in God. Not what man says about God. If I reasoned my understanding of God by my own thoughts or what someone else thought, I would not be looking to God. I would be no different from those who walk outside of what God has given to us. Looking back, when I thought about who God was to me as I was growing up, I was looking at who I thought God was and not according to the knowledge I could have through reading the Word of God. I needed to change my thinking. I realized that to live for God, I needed to change the context of my life. I did not have this understanding before. Sadly, as I see it, most people live this way.

Until I decided to follow our Lord, I had relied strictly on the way people said I should live. Certainly, I trusted my parents until I saw differently. They cared only about their own thoughts. I then began to listen to what those in the field of education taught and that seemed reasonable until philosophy classes. I even began to trust what I saw on the news until I realized they too were fomenting distrust and error. But after I decided to follow our Lord (at the age of 25), I began to see what Scripture says. I decided not to rely on the way people said, based on their reasoning and thoughts, but instead on the way God would have us to live. This was a difficult change. It is difficult because even though you believe you are right, you may not be right according to what God has said.

So I began to rely on God instead of the people I had learned from and grown with. I had not learned to rely on God being around these people. I had learned to rely on what was said by the people themselves. So changing my thinking was not easy after spending the first twenty-five years of my life wandering away from God. Even if I had listened to those who sought God, who were around me (at college for example) they had their own or their denomination's interpretations of who God was to them. They relied on what men said about Scripture. They did not realize that because God wrote Scripture, God had given specific instructions for us that could be understood. Instead, they made God the pinnacle of a religious interpretation, making God what people say He is. This is totally against Scripture! In fact, the Scriptures point this out! We simply cannot make God into our own image. Remember, Israel was rejected for this very thing.

It is no wonder most people say Scripture is a myth— incomprehensible and full of contradictions and hate. They say God is not the God of love, but of envy and evil. Or that we can make God into whomever we desire. Well, when you do just as those who were caught in their error did in the Old Testament certainly, you will think this way. Most conclude that Scripture does not matter and there is no such thing as God! Those who say things like this do not know God.

Everyone I spoke with outside of the church of Christ concerning who God is refused to look at Scripture and study what Scripture actually says. This seems to be due to their reasoning, indoctrination, and unwillingness to learn. These people were very certain of their own convictions.

Because of their certainty, they were unable to reason that we are not our own, and that our lives begin and end with God. These people based their belief in God on what they thought their faith is instead of what God has given to us in His Word. I had to move on because their belief in God was not based on knowledge. These people—friends, acquaintances, my mother, my dad, my brothers, my sisters—did not believe in God. They justified their position based on what they reasoned in their own minds. Life was about doing their own things in their own ways and God is an addendum to them. The way of God ultimately does not matter and this is wrong. Life was and still is about surviving, seeking out pleasure and just living as they saw fit. According to them, life has nothing to do with what God has said.

Everyone reconciles the way God would have them live with their own ability to reason and not with what God has given to us in His Word. Why?

What I have learned over the years, I think my friends and family believe this because the way of God is not easily trusted today. Humanity is a product of many generations of unbelief over thousands of years. Remember, the Lord was with us in person and collectively we still did not believe in Him! We are more inclined to hold to our thoughts about God, especially when we choose to ignore God. This does not excuse anyone, mind you.

Most people have a tendency not to trust in what God has given to us in His Word of truth. Those who live outside of that truth do not understand that we are not our own. They do not understand that this world is not our final abode. They have no faith in God. People who believe according to their own standards are unwilling to search for the truth of God. For the most part, my friends and family were definitely in that category.

After my baptism, when I was new to the faith, I often interacted with family and friends who were very sure of what they said about God. What could I say to their unbelief, not knowing Scripture and having only zeal?

(By the way, having zeal is not a crime, as some would have you believe. Having zeal without knowledge is not a sin. You just keep learning. Being young in the faith of God is not a sin either. It is an important time in the growth of a person who has decided to take on living for God. Older Christians need to teach and mold those who have zeal.)

I knew I was baptized for the forgiveness of my sins, but I could not clearly articulate why I was living the way God desires all people to live. I did not understand how to live that way. I needed to learn, and only a few older Christians were willing to teach me.

After being born again, I found it difficult to reason the Scriptures. What Jesus said in John 3:5 did not immediately sink in with me. I understood what Acts 2:38 said, and I had done my best to repent and be baptized. But the fact that I needed to born of water and the Spirit and become dead to sin, as Paul says in Romans 6, was not so clear for me. Even though it is clearly stated! I knew the words of our Lord were important, but I was not looking to the Word to find reasoning for my salvation, even though I was saved. I could not reason the context I was reading.

What Paul said in Romans 12:2 did not resonate with my reasoning for many years. I was too involved in just trying to survive. I was going to college and then trying to live in the ways of world, competing with those who did not know God. I soon began to build my family. Reconciling myself to all God has given was an impossible task until I made a choice.

Over the years I made the decision to rededicate myself and my family to living as I knew was right. I took the time and little by little as I studied, I began to renew my mind even more. I began to see my faith in God grow again. The fact that my faith in God grew as I looked to the Word was worth all the time and effort required.

When I decided to rededicate myself to learning about God, I gave up living as the rest of the world does and put a lot of effort into learning about God and having trusting faith. I began writing extensively about things as they were and reconciling the way of God to them. I wanted to be a better person. I wanted to be a better husband and father! I wanted to be like Abraham. I set out on my journey so to speak and here I am today. Here we are. Even as people and brethren could not reconcile what I had done to what they were seeing I trusted God would see us through this difficult time I placed us in because I was determined to learn how to be a better servant of God, husband, and father. It was a constant battle, and I constantly fell short as I tried to be a better Christian and father.

I thank God every day for my wife's commitment to me. Our love and devotion continues to grow. I am thankful for our children. They have made my life on this earth more than I ever could have imagined. I am not going to lie, these times have been an incredible struggle, and I was diagnosed with multiple sclerosis to make matters even more difficult, but it has taught me patience. I always knew and reassured my wife that God would provide as long as we kept our faith in God, and here we are.

I learned a lot by doing this renewal of my mind. To understand God, we should begin where Jesus begins and not pick and choose where we want to start. We need to understand the world we live in is not our eternal home! We need to understand there is an eternity. God desires us to come back to Him! Jesus is the way we get back to God. He is the sacrifice to God for our sin. Salvation is in Christ, and to Him we must look to understand our need to follow God. How much more clearly does it need to be said that we will not inherit the Kingdom of God unless we are born of water and the Spirit?

This is where faith in God comes in. We have always needed

to trust in God. We should not be ashamed of the gospel of our Lord. In the gospel of Christ, we see the power of God's salvation for all people. We are to live by faith in God. If we pay attention to God according to Scripture, we will be able to see His invisible attributes and His eternal power.

But this we do not do. Instead, we have our excuses. We justify ourselves so as not to glorify God or the truth. So it is that most people have their foolish hearts darkened. They become fools who profess wisdom, but this according to men (see Rom. 1).

Because the disbelievers of God live rightly in their own eyes, God has given them over to their vile passions. Woman have exchanged natural use for what is against nature. Men, leaving the natural use of women, burn in their lust for one another. They commit that which is shameful and receive the penalty of their error. This manner is becoming less shameful as sin rules the day.

Those who do these things live according to their own desires, ignoring God. So God gives them over to do those things that are wrong. These people are filled with unrighteousness, sexual immorality, wickedness, covetousness, maliciousness, envy, murder, strife, deceit, and evil-mindedness. They are backbiters and haters of God. They are violent, proud, boastful, disobedient, undiscerning, untrustworthy, unloving, unforgiving, and unmerciful. They know God and His righteousness but ignore what God has laid at our feet. I know and care for people who are very close to me who are this way, and I am certain you do too.

What these people refuse to see is that from God it is said these who practice such things are deserving of death. This is what Paul told the Romans in Romans 1. Paul was inspired by God. We need to listen.

As the created of God and Christ's own, we are not to live in the way of revelry. We should not live ashamed of the gospel of our salvation either (see Rom. 1:16). We are to live according to the Spirit of Truth. Our Lord said we should let not our hearts be troubled, but rather believe in God. Jesus said He is the "way, the truth, and the life. No one comes to the Father except through Me" (see Jn. 14:6). Further, Jesus said, "If you had known Me, you would have known My Father also; and from now on you know Him and have seen Him" (John 14:7). Jesus also said, "If you love Me, keep My commandments" (John 14:15). When we live in the way Jesus has said, "I will pray to the Father, and the Father will give us another helper— the Spirit of Truth, whom the world cannot receive, because it neither sees Him nor knows Him; but you know Him, "for He dwells with you and will be in you" (John 14:16–17).

Jesus said of this, "I will never leave you orphans; I will come to you" (John 14:18). But of those who live of the world, Jesus said, "He who does not love Me does not keep My words; and the word which you hear is not Mine, but the Father's who sent Me" (John 14:24).

Thus, in the life we live in the flesh, we are to live in the Spirit of God. We are to live just as those who trusted in God (see Heb. 11) and considered the days of their lives on this earth to be as those of travelers. We live with an expectant hope for a better place!

We can either live as those who ignore what God has given to us and believe this life is all we have, or we can "walk in the Spirit and not fulfill the lust of the flesh" (see Gal. 5.16) because, as Paul the apostle of our Lord tells the Galatians, "the flesh lusts against the Spirit" of God, and the Spirit of God is against the flesh, these being contrary to one another (see Gal. 5.17).

Though Paul is speaking to the Galatians regarding the old law, it is nevertheless true that if we live according to the Spirit of God, we will live according to how God desires us to live. This is what is meant by being born of the Spirit. We all need to live in this manner, as God has always wanted us to trust Him. We must take action!

Accordingly, then for us to understand the difference between living as we desire and living according to how God desires us to live, we need to know what it means to live according to the flesh. The world we occupy is only our abode until we get back to God. For us to live as God desires and come back to Him, we must repent, die to sin, and live according to the Spirit of God. Use Acts 2:38, Romans 6, and Galatians 5 for reference.

Whether we die to sin or go on living in our fleshly lusts, we will meet our God. If we live with God as our context, our hope should be set on being right with God. Our understanding of this is contingent upon our believing in God through our Lord and Savior. Our understanding comes through the apostles, who have instructed us by way of the Word. God has not left us empty-handed. He has "given us all things that pertain to life and godliness, through the knowledge of Him who called us by glory and virtue, by which have been given to us exceedingly great and precious promises, that through these you may be partakers of the divine nature, having escaped the corruption that is in the world through lust" (2 Pet. 1:3–4).

Today, this is certainly not understood. Most of our society is wholly given to the desires of men and what is called "democracy," not to what God has given to us. This way of living should not be. We should be smarter than this. God exists, but we just do not believe in Him as we should. We consider our lives to begin and end with this earth and what we desire. We do not trust in God. We believe this world is all there is to our living. But it isn't. Our lives continue on, just as God has said.

Understanding Scripture is almost impossible for those who believe we are the beginning and ending of all that life is. We are not. God is the beginning and ending. Nearly every person alive thinks they are right according to how they think. Money, power, and self-righteousness become what they covet. When we act this way, the way of God is far from us.

Most people could not care less that they do not know God. That is how I was. The adversary of God had me right where he wanted me. The state of mind Adam and Eve were in when they ate of the forbidden fruit is the state in which most of us live. We push the limits of what is right living according to our traditions or desires. We are unwilling to submit to God.

The Israelites are a great example of this mindset. This is why they are our example. A reading of the Old Testament will tell you this. Quite frankly, it is our selfish desire that drives us. But just because you covet something does not make your covetousness right. When we are young, this is the trap we fall into. When we are older, we decide who we are on the basis of "I have earned this." We forget that God is right there, waiting for us. Our covetousness exists because of our lack of trust in what God has given to us.

There really is no submission to God. Percentage-wise, I would say 99.99 percent of people do not serve our God as He has given. Study Scripture before you say differently. Even when people say they submit to God and indeed call themselves Christians, most make assertions not supported by the Word of God. Let me give you some examples. Where has God authorized denominations of the church Jesus gave His life for? He has not. There is not one verse in the Bible that says humans can take what Jesus gave His life for and worship God as they see fit. The church is Christ's (see Matt. 16:18 and Rom. 16:16).

Through studying God's Word I have realized that what God thinks about life is much more than what we believe we know about life. God created life, and we need to listen. God created everything. Those things that are "authorized" according to man-made decree are mostly not what God has given to us.

Consider the Catholic Church and the man called the pope. There is nothing in Scripture, which we have had for thousands of years, that gives man this authority to step into what Christ died to accomplish. Christ alone is our intercessor with God, and the church our Lord began is wholly His. Our Lord authorized the apostles to teach us. He gave no such authority to any man called the pope. There is no authorization given by our Lord for anyone to be a pope or to start a denomination professing Christ in anyone else's name. Remember, "Nor is there salvation in any other, for there is no other name under heaven given among men by which we must be saved" (Acts 4:12).

But people constantly try to make this world our home according to our traditions, just as the Jews did. However, Scripture teaches us that whether we live for God or live to our own desires, we are only sojourners on this earth. Therefore, we need to abstain from fleshly lusts, which war against the soul (see 1 Pet. 2:11). We better get our lives right because one day we are leaving!

To this end, it has been written for us to seek first the Kingdom of God (see Matt. 6:33). This applies both to leaders and those who are led. Everyone needs to seek God—rich or poor, big or small, male or female. As God so loved the world, we are to love one another (see John 3:16 and Matt. 22:37–39). God is not who you make Him out to be. God doesn't need you to make Him up. He is not an idol that needs people to say who He is. God has given us His Word, and we can know it (see Jude 3).

It is no wonder our country and our world are in constant disarray. People destroy themselves for lack of knowledge and faith (see Hosea 4:6). The faithless always tend toward the love of self instead of understanding the good things that God has done for us and how to live as He has given to us. We need to learn how to serve more!

Certainly, if you were to take the time to read God's Word, you would, believe it or not, begin to understand that God has given us over to ourselves (see Rom. 1:24). You would see this and perhaps change your life to live for God. I could only hope. We need to thank God for those who preach and teach the Word of God. Even through all of the noise of divisive behavior, the Word of God is still with us. There are still people willing to teach the truth in God's Word according to Scripture—not many, though.

As I was growing up, I did not know anything about God. I did not see that living without any knowledge of God—drunk, fornicating, and lascivious—was wrong. I did not consider that I needed to know about God or to be there for anyone. I thought I was right in all I did. Doing what was actually right by God did not matter to me because I did not know what was right.

Growing up, I had no convictions. I only went along for the ride. All I did or wanted to do was all that mattered. I did not know where I was going or that my life had any specific meaning. I just existed. I believe that is the way it is for most people. My parents never taught me about our God, and their parents never taught them.

As a teenager, I learned that when people placed rules upon you, it was your right to be as disobedient as you liked. Similarly, you can hear the cries and screams from we the people who have deemed that all we would like to do is our right to do. We are babies who do not know any differently, and this is allowed. We shame and even punish people for trying to discipline others according to righteous behavior. But when I yelled at my mother and said I hated her, I never considered that God was watching me.

Well, though my parents were unwilling to punish me for my behavior, God was still watching. The very same morning I told my mother I hated her, I got in a bicycle accident and ended up in a coma for three weeks, partially paralyzed! My life changed in that instance. At the time I did not care for instruction or know that I needed to care. I was a product of the environment my parents and society had created for me. I was all that mattered, and I was determined to do what I wanted, regardless of what anyone thought. Why couldn't I do what I wanted? I was in charge of myself, wasn't I?

After my accident, I began to see things differently. I was forced to look at life differently. I was dependent upon others for help. I had to learn how to talk, walk, read, and write all over again. Looking back, I dare say my mother was not thoughtful of my needs as I was healing. I was fourteen years old, and I needed a tutor to help me learn at home because I could not go to school. My mother didn't try to teach me because she did not know how, and I do not know that I would have listened anyway. I was forced into a new way of living my life. All of my worldly hopes and dreams had been made more difficult.

Oddly, it was at this time that I began to see the difference between right and wrong. Perhaps reason began to come to me. I saw divisions even though people were screaming about unity. I could see people were selfish and mean. They desired only things that felt good to them and did not care about those who enforce the law. I saw this among teenagers mostly. Just read God's Word and you will see why. Parents, and that now includes me, have dropped the ball. When parents give up, children lose out and so does the rest of the world.

Nevertheless, I began to question what I had believed to be correct up to that point, and I did not know why. I still desired that which was wrong. I did not know any differently. But I was changing. I was beginning to grow in my understanding. I was beginning to take the time to learn. This was something I had never done before.

I saw there was very little unity even within my own family, only a sense of division as we grew. Our family did not care for one another the way we should have, the way God desires. Each of us justified our every action according to our own standard and not the standard of God. We did not believe that love meant serving one another. We were and remain very different.

Even our neighbors did not reach out to one another. In fact, a denominational preacher who lived across the street from us shot and killed our little dog as we children watched from the bus stop! What did this say to our family about a so-called "man of God"? None of us were united as people created in the image of God. We all did our own things and were at times hostile to things that were good.

For an example, my family did not like some nice people who lived down the street from us. They never seemed to have any troubles or cause any problems. One morning, trying to find a friend for my sister because we were new to the area, I pulled a knife on the neighbor girl at her front door because she would not play with my sister! In another instance, someone who I thought was a friend tried to shoot me with a BB gun because I went to visit him. I thought we were friends. Indeed we are friends today, at least on social media, and I am thankful for this. But you can see that without understanding God and being taught according to His truth, we are divided!

Our wisdom cannot unify all the different desires and cultures or insist upon the definition of what is sinful and wrong, because that which is of sin to God is lawful to us. We make all things lawful—or at least right in our own eyes. There is a difference, but we just do not know this. We live this way because we desire the way of humanity over what God has given to us.

Our leaders cry out about "unity in diversity," trying to make this the mantra of our lives instead of the Word of God. We need to be united by God! How can we unite in our diversity? How can mankind define right and wrong by their own measure and still expect to live in the manner God has given? For a great example of this kind of thinking, look at Jeffrey Epstein, Nancy Pelosi, Adam Schiff, Alexandria Ocasio-Cortez, Hillary and Bill Clinton, Barak Obama, the WHO and those with whom they associate. Look at Jimmy Swaggart, Joel Osteen, and Joyce Meyer.

Why are most people so devoted to the famous, the child molesters, the welfare recipients of the elite political class, the liars, the thieves, the false teachers, and the murderers? Why do they not care about things that are correct? Why don't they care about the things of God? Instead, they live their lives according to their selfish ambition and hate. If they are not in charge, then things must be wrong, and everything about what is right must be subverted until they have succeeded!

According to "we the people," what is even considered correct? Is democracy correct? What about the law of Christ? (See Matt. 22:36–39.) Who gave men and women this authority? But this is how we live, and so we must, for the sake of living peacefully, succumb to those who care little for civility and what is right with God. Today, the unjust, the unrighteous are held in high esteem by a certain group of leaders who throw away the law for what they call social equality. However, this so called equality only comes from denying others the right to live peacefully. How is that right?

Needless to say, we are in a losing battle with the adversary. We allow every whim to be right and never hold anyone accountable for wrongdoing. Consider the teaching of homosexuality to our children and the resultant pedophilia. Sin has grasped our children, and the public schools are ripe with what comes from this seed. Unfortunately, there are those who are too abusive of what is right by God. Barack Obama comes to mind here and his fostering of the LGBTQ movement. This movement is against all God has given to us. Pete Buttigieg will never be right in the sight of God as long as he is a homosexual.

The more I studied what God has given to us, the more I saw how God defines sin. Over many years, I realized that I did not want any part of what all of these people were doing. It is no wonder most people do not want God's Word taught in the public arena. People do not love God because they do not know God, and they do not want to be constrained in any way. They reject the good of God because they love the things of the world and the pleasures of this life.

People desire what is right in their own eyes, just as it is written in the book of Judges. This is because of their self-righteous pursuit of what they deem to be right. The entertainment industry shows us this. By definition, there is no unity in diversity, and we are all very diverse in our division. There is only chaos. Tolerance becomes the thing people have to hold to.

The leaders of our land force by law all the things that God has stated are wrong, just so we can have a little glimpse of civility. But still, the cries continue especially if those who try to do what is right stray even a little off the right path. Sin is the reason. Each of us needs to recognize our responsibility not to be part of continuing what is wrong.

Still, we must love our neighbor as ourselves to fulfill the law of Christ. This applies to all people, regardless of what our desires are. Hate the sin, love the sinner.

Let me be clear when I say the law of the land is the law and must be followed, unless it goes against what God has given to us. God did say vengeance is His and He will repay (see Rom. 12:19). I wish I could let God have what He said was His!

Those who are charged with enforcement of what is right are coming to an end due to those who have powerful monetary backing and cry that our democracy is in peril. What did I say about this type of fearmongering? Christ's own must be wise as serpents and gentle as doves as we learn our role in life (see Matt. 10:16). Our lives are changing, and this is strictly because of what the adversary has brought to the world. The fear mongers are out to change the face of the world and have the money to do it. It seems we are powerless to stop this force as even the elect are swept away into this error (see Matt. 24.24). The love of money is the root of all evil (1 Tim. 6:10).

We should never forget what God has given to us: "But the fruit of the Spirit is love, joy, peace, longsuffering, kindness, goodness, faithfulness, gentleness, self-control. Against such there is no law. And those who are Christ's have crucified the flesh with its passions and desires. If we live in the Spirit, let us also walk in the Spirit" (Gal. 5:22–25). Senseless rioting and killing of the innocent does not accomplish this!

I realize it is hard to grasp how we must live according to God and not according to what we desire. This is why I am writing. I want everyone to understand what God relayed to us through His Word.

Ultimately, we left God and Jesus is the only way for us to get back to God. God gave us this ability, and we even have the enduring Word of God to continually guide us. We have what we need to bring our lives back to being correct with God. We need to reconcile our lives to God (see 2 Cor. 5:20). God wants us to be with Him because He loves us. We are to be sinless as we were before the adversary took the innocence of Eve and Adam by deception. When we live this way, born again of water and the Spirit, then we will understand this world is not our home and know our eternal abode is with God.

10

My Coworker

NATURALLY, WHEN I began to read what God had prepared for us, I saw that the things the Bible said were different from what I had been raised to believe life is. I saw the need I had to make a change in my life. The story of our Lord and His apostles took hold of me. They stood for the truth of God and yet were ridiculed and punished for the good news that God gave to the world. People hated what was good, for the simple reason that it was good. I knew I needed to learn more.

I was not so far gone as to claim I knew the truth of life. Nor was I so comfortable in how I was living to say I knew the way everything should be. I didn't know that way, and so I wanted to learn more. I saw what was written in the Word of God was different then how I was living, but I was not willing to make the commitment to living for a way of life I did not understand.

I began to read the Word of God and I began to understand the way people are today is how they have always been. I began to see a manner of life that made sense to me. As I read the Bible, I learned the truth about how man has continued to lean on his own understanding, in ignorance of God. I read how God has been patiently waiting for us to reconcile our lives to Him. Knowing this, I began to focus on what mattered. I learned it was not within people to direct their own footsteps (see Jer. 10:23). But we sure love to go this way and never realize we are on the wrong path.

Ralph, my biblically smart coworker, and I had Bible studies at work during our lunch breaks. I was comfortable with this. But the time came for me to start living for God instead of just listening to words. That made me a little uncomfortable. It took me three months to come to the realization that I needed to be baptized (application of John 3:5). I began to make the changes I needed, but I was not fully obedient. I made the confession of my faith in God because I believed in God and what He gave to us. I did not understand all of what God gave to us, nor what it all meant, but I did believe a man died for us so that we could be raised in newness of life. It was at this time I was baptized and I died to sin (see Rom. 6). Again, I did not completely understand all of the significance of baptism or what it meant to live as God would have us live, but I was on my way to learning about God and building my faith. Ultimately, I believed Jesus is the Son of God.

This is why we read and study what God has given to us. People teach for this reason. We do this so we can know God! This is why we need to change our manner of life. To be one with God, we need to come back to the Kingdom of God. We need to do as He commands (see John 14:15).

Today, after twenty-five years of studying God's Word, I submit willingly to the commandment of God and trust His every word. I do my best to put myself behind what God wants from me and from us. I take the time to learn and teach. It's not always convenient or accepted, but it is necessary. I work the will of God because that is what God expects of everyone on the earth. God wants us to follow Him, but I know based on secular history and the biblical record that men and women are always going to do what they want and believe what they desire. Only a few will submit themselves to our God.

I told my friend the carpenter (who, like me, was not biblically smart) that I had discovered the difference between faith and belief. I told him where I had found the truth, but he was not interested in taking it any further. It was a good exercise of thought, but perhaps an overwhelming task to put God where he had not had God before. Why is this so difficult?

I guess I was searching for more, and so I was more open to hearing the truth of our lives. I did not know it at the time, but when I was presented with the opportunity to learn, I took it. Unfortunately for the carpenter, he was just another one of my friends or family who did not want to understand the entire significance of putting God first.

This was when I began to trust in God. This in itself was an odd thing for me to do. I had never trusted many people. Why was it that I trusted what I was being told from a book about someone who called Himself God? Especially when I had never really cared about anything or anyone? Perhaps my interest in the things of God were because I had always been searching for something and never found any concrete knowledge. I could never say I understood what I needed to know in life to live right. After all, what did it mean to live right? Wasn't that a subjective area we could each form our own opinion about?

Over time, I learned something important. I had been left stranded to learn about God because of the many who had gone before me and neglected what God has given to us all. We the people have done all we can to keep God to ourselves or take God out of the way. Either we do not know any differently or are just too selfish to realize how great life is as God's people. Above all, it seems we the people decided God does not exist. We think little about helping everyone to know that we have a God and He lives for us!

Publishing what I am writing right now is one of the ways I am seeking to help people realize their need to come to God. I wonder how it will go? I know I will do my best to get the mainstream to publish what I have written, but we will see what they will do. Will I be rejected or accepted? Will people believe what is written? Will they consider their need to come to God even a little? I do not know. What I do know is that if I have the ability to help someone for the good, and I choose not to help, then I am no good to anyone. "Therefore, to him who knows to do good and does not do it, to him it is sin" (James 4:17). I do not want to be against what God has created.

Thank God for the coworker who decided to help me understand the Word of God. Because of his efforts, my wife, our son, his wife, our daughter, her friends, our friends, and many others have been encouraged to keep seeking God. Ultimately, they need to make the decision to serve our God. We are all different, but we have all been baptized to die to sin. Therefore we are to live within the Spirit God has given to us. Our Lord is our focus. If you think about it, a lot has come from that little question I decided to follow up on. Renewing your mind to God is difficult, but as I have proven, it can be done.

11

It Was My Faith

ONCE I LEARNED about God, my devotion began to change. This is what repentance is. Unfortunately all of my past associations dissolved as I began to live according to the truth of God. I say unfortunately because my friends wanted nothing to do with what I had learned. The common factor with those whom I associated was their devotion to what they had always known.

I grew out of the weekend revelry that took my money and kept me from growing my faith in God or even becoming a good person. I was choosing to grow in the knowledge of our Lord and my parents, brothers, sisters, and friends did not want to be a part of what I had learned. They had their own ideas about life and God. They did not care to find out the truth of our lives. Like most people, they were not willing to look at the Word of God. There was within them a singular desire to hold on to their own thoughts about God. They, just as I was need to renew their minds to God. They did not want to do this but, isn't this what we are taught by the Scriptures of God? (see Rom. 12.2).

I had a lot of changing to do. As I would realize many years later, I had a lot of baggage to let go of. I made these changes willingly because I had been saved by the blood of Jesus. I had died to sin, just as Jesus commanded and Scripture taught. I was motivated to live for a man who I believed was born of God and who died to take away my sin—even though I was not entirely certain what this meant. I needed to make a change.

That is why I kept studying. I needed to know God. I believed in God, but I did not understand everything I needed to know. Early on, as I was growing in my faith, I was encouraged to keep studying by faithful brethren who cared about me. They urged me not to become discouraged. Not all of my brethren did this. Not all of them cared. Some were very discouraging to me. I looked past this and kept my faith going because it was not my brethren who died for me. It was Jesus who died for us and was raised again. But I have to say their encouragement sure would have helped me along the way.

Jesus is the One we all need to serve. When we live this way, we are living correctly. If your brethren are not the way you think they should be, you need to keep on living as God and Jesus have given. God and Jesus are who matter, after all is considered.

> "But what things were gain to me, these I have counted loss for Christ. Yet indeed I also count all things loss for the excellence of the knowledge of Christ Jesus my Lord, for whom I have suffered the loss of all things, and count them as rubbish, that I may gain Christ and be found in Him, not having my own righteousness, which is from the law, but that which is through faith in Christ, the righteousness which is from God by faith; that I may know Him and the power of His resurrection, and the fellowship of His sufferings, being conformed to His death, if, by any means, I may attain to the resurrection from the dead.' (Phil. 3:7–11)

Understanding who God is was something I needed to do and learn. Who else could grow my faith for me and learn what it means to be born of the Spirit of God? It was my job to understand who our God is. The preacher is there to help us see what God has given to us, but we each have the individual responsibility to become what God would have us be.

Among the denominational teachings or even the way of what men have conjured, this seems to be a job that only a "special" person with a college degree can do. It is not. The truth of the matter is that once you become a child of God according to John 3.5, you can teach if you are able. There is no special synod you need to attend or college degree you need to study for. You can preach. Know what God says about this though. You should develop public speaking skills and understand your Bible to deliver a message to a congregation, but teaching other people about God is a task all men and women who have done as John 3:5 says need to be doing a lot more of. Being a teacher of God is a much-needed job in our lost and dying world. This is why we study and grow our faith. You certainly do not need to be what the pope claims. You do need to do as God has said though.

So I studied, and what I learned was that if I desired to be one with God, I could not live my life without doing what our Lord has asked us to do. My friend Ralph taught me the gospel of our Lord, and I could read that submission to God was essential to being with God. Jesus says, "If you love Me, obey My commandments" (John 14:15). I learned I needed to be obedient to God and that I was loved by God, as is clearly stated in John 3:16. What an amazing concept—I could die to sin and live with God! Even I could be buried with Christ and this through baptism to be raised in newness of life (see Rom. 6:4).

I was ready to give up my life of chaos and human desire to live for a man who said He was God and had come to take away my sins. Imagine being loved so much and being able to come to God and know the purpose of your life. A man actually died as a sacrifice to God for us! What kind of love was this? I needed to learn more.

The apostle Paul said that when we are baptized, we are buried with Christ. Just as Jesus was raised from the dead by the glory of the Father, we too will walk in newness of life when we are baptized (see Rom. 6). Our Lord and Savior Jesus Christ made this possible. Everyone has this opportunity. All we need to do is know God and take advantage of what God has freely given to us through His Son. All who do so will be resurrected when our God calls us home.

How do I know this? Why am I so certain this is the truth? Scripture is clear: when we crucify the old body of sin through baptism, we will be dead to sin. We who have died to sin have been freed from sin. We are no longer to obey sin in its lusts. Read Romans 6 and understand what it means to live according to the Spirit of God. Instead of living our lives aimlessly, we are to present ourselves unto the righteousness of God. We are to renew our minds and do the will of God. This is what repentance is! This is being born of the Spirit! After baptism, our desires should be to live for God and seek all things according to God's Word. We must free ourselves from the bondage of sin that we may walk in newness of life.

God be thanked for His enduring love and mercy, because without them we would not have the time to learn about God, do His will, and save ourselves from this perverse generation (see Acts 2:40).

Our obvious lack of faith in and understanding of our salvation says a lot about who we are, what we do not care about, and all we have ignored concerning who our God is over the centuries. We rely on those who tell us soothing words, (Joel Osteen) who teach error, and who preach against what Scripture actually says for their own purpose. Generation after generation has not been able to conceptualize what God has done for us because of this.

So the questions arise: Why should I believe in God? What do I believe about God? Because of these questions many different creeds have been formed and what men and women believe is the truth about what God has said has been taught. Every bit of what they teach is error if it does not conform to the Word of God.

When we read God's Word, we see that God is the source of all truth (see John 14:6). We will read we cannot add to God's Word and be correct (see Deut. 29:29). We will see that God is love (see 1 John 4:7) and without the love of God, we are lost. It is not an insignificant thing that people have willingly looked away from God, placing their focus on what man says and not what God says. Should we not then have this same love in us that God has for us? What about having the love of others within us too? This kind of love takes work. It takes a lot of study and prayer. Submitting ourselves to God and to others and praying in all things are not easy. My life is proof that this is the case.

Remember, I did not learn anything about God from my parents, nor did I think about who God is on my own. It was not by or through my own understanding that I know who God is or that I have been saved. No! I heard the commandment of our Lord, instructing His apostles to baptize in the name of the Father, Son, and Holy Spirit. My coworker Ralph taught me that Jesus taught His apostles to observe "all things that I have commanded you" (Matt. 28:20a). Therefore, I have learned what it means to be saved because of the bondservants of Jesus Christ. Paul said, "For just as you presented your members as slaves of uncleanness, and of lawlessness leading to more lawlessness, so now present your members as slaves of righteousness for holiness" (Rom. 6:19).

Our purpose in this life above all other things is to renew our minds to God. This is how we are born of the Spirit! The apostle Paul was clear about this in his letter to the Romans. He also said in Ephesians, "For by grace you have been saved through faith, and that not of yourselves; salvation is the gift of God, not of works, lest anyone should boast" (Eph. 2:9–10).

Our salvation is a gift. God did not have to give us a way to be saved, but God did through His Son, Jesus. When we obey our

Lord through baptism, we die to sin, but we must live to God also (see Eph. 2:8; John 14:15; Acts 2:38; Rom. 6; John 3:5).

Question: What about Hebrews 11? If our salvation is a gift of God, then why must we die to sin to enter the Kingdom of God?

Answer: Read John 3 and Romans 6. Do not be deceived by those who say we are saved by faith only. It is true that we have salvation and that it is a gift from God. But it is not true that God's gift of salvation means we do not need to be buried with Christ in baptism to die to sin. That would not go along with the rest of Scripture. Don't get me wrong, our faith is necessary, just as it was for Abraham. Abraham obeyed God to be found righteous. So if we believe we can live by faith alone and not obedient faith, we are misinformed. Even Jesus was obedient to God. Remember Jesus told his disciples that if they loved Him, they would obey His commandments (see John 14:15).

Necessarily, obedient faith is actionable. If you do not do as God has said, how can you say you are living according to the Spirit of God? Hebrews 11 tells the story of how faith moved people to live by the faith they proclaimed. Even Jesus was baptized. Since He is the Author of our salvation, shouldn't we be baptized also?

Jesus instructed His disciples to go and teach, baptizing in the name of the Father, the Son, and the Holy Spirit. We need to listen to what has been written and obey the commandment. We do not even have to guess if this is true! The act of baptism and its importance is described over and over in Scripture.

In Romans 6, Paul reiterates what baptism does for us: we die to sin so we may be raised in newness of life. We must never forget this. Yet this instruction is made out to be a lie by many who claim to be teachers of the Word of God. They teach error. Read your Bible to understand the truth. There is no salvation if you are not buried with Christ in baptism. How can you be resurrected to newness of life if you have not died to sin and lived to God? We must trust what God has given to us. Our eternal life depends on our faith in God.

12

Study to Know the Context of Our Lives

THERE ARE MANY well-intentioned and not so well-intentioned people who only believe in God and think that only their "faith" will save them. This is not true at all. Faith without works is dead (see James 2:18). Therefore, for our faith to save us, it must move us to obey God.

> Thus also faith by itself, if it does not have works, is dead. But someone will say, "You have faith, and I have works." Show me your faith without your works, and I will show you my faith by my works. You believe that there is one God. You do well. Even the demons believe—and tremble! But do you want to know, O foolish man, that faith without works is dead? Was not Abraham our father justified by works when he offered Isaac his son on the altar? Do you see that faith was working together with his works, and by works faith was made perfect? And the scripture was fulfilled which says, "Abraham believed God, and it was accounted to him for righteousness." And he was called the friend of God. You see then that a man is justified by works, and not by faith only.

> Likewise, was not Rahab the harlot also justified by works when she received the messengers and sent them out another way? For as the body without the spirit is dead, so faith without works is dead also. (James 2:17–26)

Think about the act of faith. If we believe in God, we should do the works of God. Hebrews 11 shows us this very thing. I believe in God and this is why I am writing! Consider, if we believe our parents, we will obey them right? Mental ascent is not the same as having faith. Obedience to the faith is what the context of our lives should be. Our belief in God needs to propel us to act, or else what we call our belief and our faith are only thoughts. We can think about things all we like, but if our thoughts of God do not produce action, we will not be one with our God! Therefore our faith is to be built on what God has told us.

So when God tells us we have something to do, it is not a choice for us—if we would like to remain in God's favor. Remember, Jesus said, "If you love Me, obey My commandments" (John 14:15). Adam and Eve are a great example here. When they disobeyed God, they were removed from the garden and all of humanity began to die. They were punished for their disobedience to God. Their belief in God did not bring them to obey God, and they sinned. Adam and Eve needed to obey God to be right with God, and so do we. When Jesus came, He did not change the fact we need to obey God. In fact, Jesus made it explicitly clear if we do not obey God, we are lost.

> "He who has My commandments and keeps them, it is he who loves Me. And he who loves Me will be loved by My Father, and I will love him and manifest Myself to him" (John 14:21).

When we sin, we separate ourselves from God. This is why we need to die to sin and be renewed in our minds, to live according to the Spirit of God. If we do not live according to what God has said, our spirit will be dead even as alive as we may feel.

Any teaching of God that does not conform to what God has said is not right. One such teaching is being saved before baptism. This teaching is incorrect. As I have said before, denominationalism teaches erroneous doctrines concerning our common salvation. What humans create about God does not change how God has determined for us to be saved. We need to follow every word of Scripture for us to be right with God. The pope, for example, has no authority to speak on behalf of God unless the pope's words are in accordance with God's Word. The pope is not the head of the church. Christ is the head of the church. Men can preach the Word of God, but not according to what their thoughts are. God is clear (see 2 Tim. and Rom. 15:4).

The book of John, the disciple whom Jesus loved, says that God is love. When I speak about God, I will not deceive you with my feelings or with false teaching. How can I intercede for a perfect love? I am not perfect. I am perfected in Christ through baptism (see 1 John 2.5). So I have submitted myself to God through our Lord because God's Word is clear. You cannot tell me John 3.5 is not clear and does not matter.

God's love for us is such that He sent Jesus to die so that we can be buried with Him in baptism, to be resurrected to life when He comes again. Dying to sin is the only way we can get back to God. All people need to know this. The Bible, God's Word, explains this very well.

Again, after growing up outside of who God is, and experiencing years of not living the way God desires me to live, I have changed. I am a child of God. This is where my faith is. But it is this understanding of who God is and who we are to God has become almost impossible for people to comprehend. There is always something to get in the way of what is good. Remember the adversary?

Growing up, I did not know God. This was because not one person in my life was dedicated enough to God or me to tell me about God. My mother gave all of us children a Bible when I was five years old, but she never read it with us. Neither did our dad. The first time I read it was when I was twenty-five years old. God never was of any interest to me.

Because of the way we live our lives, it has become nearly impossible to gain a clearly articulated understanding of God. There are those who ignore or adulterate the truth of God and lie about what the Word of God says and masses of people end up believing the lie. Survival becomes much more difficult when you go against God. With all of the man-made advances we see, we go further and further away from the truth of God. It is in this manner of living that we have let go of our God.

Humanity is focused on the decrees of human institutions, which do not give God the glory and instead profess a godless desire for unity through human reasoning. It is no wonder our young people do not believe in God and there are so many cultural problems. Because of doctrinal error, we believe what is factually incorrect about God and what our relationship to God needs to be. And so each generation learns something about God that they consider true which is factually false.

We must do all we can to live according to the truth of God. Surprisingly, most preachers are good at explaining this. God has given us His Word, and it has always been with us. All we need to do is look and we will find. Moses tells us this in Deuteronomy 4, and Jesus does as well in Matthew 7:7. The preacher, however, is not the person who is supposed to read God's Word for you. You are!

If our world is ever to live in harmony, it needs to live as our Creator has said. Therefore, we need to know what God has said in order to understand our purpose. Being with God is that purpose. God made life this way. This is why we must "seek first the Kingdom of God and His righteousness." (Matt. 6.33a). When we do His will, "all these things shall be added to you" (Matt. 6:33b).

We have choices to make in life. Either we choose to live with God as our context, or we choose to live as we desire and lose sight of what God desires His people to be. If we choose to live as we desire, and what we desire is not what God has given to us, then we are living out the manifest destiny of the adversary. We are outside of the protection of our God. You need only look at the chaos surrounding us to see that this is true.

We have lost the context to our lives because we do not listen to God. Nor do we study what God has made available to us. There is just too much noise in life for us to focus upon God as we should. This is not because God made our lives difficult, but because we have made it nearly impossible to understand who God is.

When you understand the context of what happened in Genesis 3, you can piece together why our lives are this way. Our understanding of who God is and what He has done for us was taken away by the adversary. Our understanding was lost to us, and our children grew up searching for something their parents should have known and taught.

There is nothing more important in our lives than knowing God and doing what He has commanded us. Your favorite TV show and the Constitution of the United States are not more important than knowing the Word of God! Because of what we believe are competing priorities we lack reasoning ability; we do not like to retain God in our knowledge (see Rom. 1:28). This is the dichotomy. We need to know God. Our children need to know our God. To know God is to know our purpose, but we do not like to know God. We love to change the rules of our lives which actually cause us to live outside of the grace of God. This is "progress" to eternal damnation.

97

Dads, I am talking to you. Your job is to train up your children in the nurture and admonition of God (see Eph. 6:4) and to love your wife (see Eph. 5:25). Unfortunately, this training does not happen according to the commandment of God. We are content to raise imbeciles who have no clue of their need to die to sin and live for the eternal purpose for which we were created. A lot of parents are more concerned with their children playing sports and showing just how great their children are at some event than learning what it means to be wholly devoted to God. God just becomes mostly an idea or someone we can place on the back burner and that is not true. It seems that moms and dads would rather have latchkey children, growing up in the public arena of daycare and public schools, living their lives in the context of what society gives them instead of what God has provided for us. While all of the things that surround us are nice, our devotion needs to be to God.

God is our eternal purpose. Our obedience to God depends upon us looking to God as the One we will give an account to. The other side of this is the context we find ourselves in today. We do not know what it is to have love that is enduring, just as our God has given to us.

God must be first among all things in our lives. He is to be our beginning and our ending (see Rev. 22:13). We need to place God first or we simply are not living as God has always desired. If we continue to live our lives with God in our back pocket so to speak, not caring for what sin is and ignore the very way that releases us from the bondage of eternal death, we will always be lost. It does not matter what we believe or who we know. If what we believe does not match what God's Word says, we are lost. We cannot ignore acts that lead us to the way of God (baptism and being born of the Spirit) and say we are okay.

Our ancestors are not going to save us. Just because your mother and your grandmother were Baptist does not mean you should be, especially after you know the truth of God. We must be buried with Christ in baptism to be His. This is how our sin is removed (see Acts 2:38, Rom. 6). We must be born again to be with God.

Just because you believe something to be true does not make it true. Unless what you believe concerning our relationship with God matches what Jesus said, you are wrong. The purpose of our Lord was to put all things in order according to the eternal purpose of God. True are the words "God so loved the world that He gave us His only begotten Son" (John 3.16a) to die for us. Jesus, God's Son, said, "Unless you are born of water and the Spirit you cannot enter the Kingdom of God." Both of these statements were made in the same conversation between Nicodemus and Jesus as recorded in John 3.

When you begin to understand who Jesus is and what He accomplished, you can see Jesus took the traditions of men (specifically Israel) and made them His own, giving them to us. As I have studied, I have determined that what Jesus did as the Son of God was to take Israel's traditions and make them His own. As the Jews used the mikveh for their ritual purity, Christ made baptism essential for the remission of sins.[7] We are not paying attention.

Our Christ did many things, but most important, He became the sacrificial Lamb of God who died upon the cross (see John 1.29, Luke 23). He made salvation easy! Because of His sacrifice, when we die to sin and live according to the Spirit of God, we are saved. Israel knew of the Messiah, and so do billions of people today. Investigate what God has given to us and come to the knowledge of the truth of God! Our baptism cleanses us to the eternal purpose of God through Jesus Christ. God wants us to

---

[7] http://www.bible.ca/synagogues/Mikvah-Christian-Maker-Baptistry-wash-sins-Architectural-ancient-Synagogue-pre-70AD-standardized-typology-design-incorporated-copied-similarities-into-church.htm

be His people, but we cannot be His people unless we die to sin. Baptism is the way.

Be understanding, because we need to live according to His Spirit and not according to what we think. Grow in the faith that was delivered to the saints. Study God's Word and do not lean on your own understanding or erroneous man-made teachings and halve truths. Remember, Christ died for His church, the congregation of people gathered together in His name. Christ did not die for the Lutheran Church or any other denomination you can think of. Our Lord died for all of us, according to His Word for our salvation.

Grow your faith by trusting our Lord (see Rom. 10:17).

13

Being Right with God

CLEARLY, GOD DOES not want us to change what He has given to us. This has been apparent since Adam and Eve in the garden of Eden. Being right with God means doing as God has said. This is faith. Remember, the adversary caused Eve to believe a lie and Moses instructs the Israelites not to add or take away from the commandments of God (see Deut. 4:2, 12:32). This is also true of what is written in the book of Revelation, which reveals that if anyone adds to the prophecy of the book of God, God will add the plagues that are written in the book (see Rev. 22:18). We cannot change what God has already given. When we do, we are wrong. Neither men nor women make God who He is. God is and always has been.

Jesus's death upon the cross is the avenue by which we get back to God. Jesus's death was of necessity, because Jesus Christ is the sacrificial Lamb of God. Hopefully you have been studying to know this truth and grow your faith.

In the Old Testament, particularly in the five books of Moses, there was a sacrificial animal (see Cain and Abel). A lamb was slain among all of the other animals to put off the sin of Israel and make atonement before God. Israel rejected God's plan for them, and God left them in silence for over four hundred years. When our Lord came, He became our Sacrificial Lamb! This is what is mean that God so loved the world that He gave us His Son!

So what did Christ's death upon the cross bring for us? The book of Hebrews tells us all that Christ did for us and you should read it. Remember, Jesus said, "Most assuredly, I say to you, unless one is born of water and the Spirit, he cannot enter the Kingdom of God" (John 3.5). This is key to our understanding of what and who God is to us. Being born of water and the Spirit is essential to our salvation! It means "to present yourselves to God as being alive from the dead, and your members as instruments of righteousness to God" (Rom. 6:14).

It is imperative we understand how God wants us to live our lives. This is why I keep repeating myself.

This should be an a-ha moment if you have not understood how you are to live your life to God. I hope what I have written helps you. Even our Lord was baptized by John, who recognized that he should not baptize our Lord. Jesus said for it to be done to "fulfill all righteousness" (Matt. 3.15) and so Jesus was baptized. Still, John knew that his place was only as a messenger (see Mark 1:1–11). John's purpose was to inaugurate the way of our Lord.

After "all righteousness was fulfilled" (Matt. 3:15), Jesus said to His disciples, "All authority has been given unto Me in Heaven and on earth. Go and make disciples of all the nations, baptizing them in the name of the Father and of the Son and the Holy Spirit, teaching them to observe all things that I have commanded you; and I am with you always, even to the end of the age" (Matt. 28:18–20).

Baptism is what now saves us (see 1 Pet. 3:21). This is after a pattern that the Jews had and Jesus made His own. (An internet search should prove enlightening if not footnote 7). This is part of how we are made right with God. We are not baptized because we are saved already, as denominationalism teaches. We are saved when we become dead to sin, to be raised in newness of life at the resurrection of Jesus Christ. We are saved when we live our lives to God.

It is this mortifying of the body of sin that is essential for our salvation. Think about it. The Jews on the day of Pentecost came together, listened to Peter and the others. and asked, "Men and brethren what should we do?" (see Acts 2.37).

Peter said, "Repent, and let everyone of you be baptized in the name of Jesus Christ for the remission of sins; and you shall receive the gift of the Holy Spirit" (Acts 2:38).

Salvation comes from being obedient to the Word of Christ. Did not Jesus tell His disciples to do this very thing? Again, look at Matthew 28. If baptism does not save us by removing our sin, then the words of the apostles of Christ, Peter and Paul, are lies, and Jesus Himself was not telling the truth! If sin does not separate us from God, then why did Adam and Eve need to go out from the presence of God? It is time to understand the basics of what God has given to us and live as God has given. Quit listening to those teachers on TV who use your money to buy mansions and jets. False teachers are everywhere, and so are those who do not believe what God has said.

I tell you these things that you may learn to believe in Jesus and His Words. That you may understand what it is to be right with God! (see John 20:30-31).

14

Speaking and Teaching Correctly

THERE IS AN unchecked desire to teach as doctrine the commandment of men among popular teachers of what we call modern-day Christianity (see Matt. 15:1-9). What they teach today is essentially unchecked error concerning how we obtain a correct relationship with our God as they add to and take away from what our Lord has given. If what is taught about our Lord is not based on the written Word of God, we cannot follow this and expect to be right with God.

For this reason I thought it necessary to reiterate the fundamentals of what the Word of God says. Especially during the last sixty years as I understand it, not to mention the error being taught since the 1st century, we have been inundated with half-truths and what amount to lies about what the Word of God says. False teaching about our God has wreaked havoc on our world. We have allowed ourselves to be indoctrinated with untruths concerning the Word of our salvation and justify ourselves by saying this is "my faith." It is time we each take the time to learn who our God is and not base our salvation on our desire for moral autonomy.

> In the beginning, God created the heavens and the earth. (Gen. 1:1)

Then God said, "Let Us make man in Our image, according to Our likeness; let them have dominion over the fish of the sea, over the birds of the air, and over the cattle, over all the earth and over every creeping thing that creeps on the earth." So God created man in His *own* image; in the image of God He created him; male and female He created them. Then God blessed them, and God said to them, "Be fruitful and multiply; fill the earth and subdue it; have dominion over the fish of the sea, over the birds of the air, and over every living thing that moves on the earth." (Gen. 1:26–28)

And Adam said: "This *is* now bone of my bones. And flesh of my flesh; She shall be called Woman, because she was taken out of Man." Therefore a man shall leave his father and mother and be joined to his wife, and they shall become one flesh. And they were both naked, the man and his wife, and were not ashamed. (Gen. 2:23–25)

Let it be recognized we have the story of our creation that has been under the stewardship of the Hebrews since before Moses. We all know the Torah exists, and in it we find the creation of mankind, our fall, and our subsequent need to come back to God. It is this last fact we do not understand, comprehend, and we deny because of and in many different ways.

God created us and all things for us. As the Word of God says, all things that were created, we have had dominion over. We even had access to the Tree of Life! (see Gen. 3:22.) But we also had access to the Tree of the Knowledge of Good and Evil (see Gen. 3:1–5). Herein was only prohibition from God: we were not to eat of the Tree of the Knowledge of Good and Evil because if we did, we would know what was good and what was evil, and we would ultimately see death. Evil separates us from God. Even just having the knowledge of what evil is separates us. Have you ever thought about this?

But of this tree we did eat. We ate at the suggestion of the tempter, the adversary of God, who is evil personified. Why? Satan is evil personified because he does not live according to the commandment of God and he seeks others to do the same. Likewise, when we do not live according to the commandment of God we are evil. What do you think the purpose of sacrifice was for? Sacrifice has always been needed throughout the Bible, it's just that God made what is required by us easy as Jesus took this burden away; except for our need to be born of water and the Spirit. This is why ignorance is not an excuse. We can know God, but we have chosen to ignore God.

We ate of the tree because our desire took over our reason. Remember this important fact. This is the key to our separation from God. The adversary of God and humankind, the Devil, is the one who enticed Eve and then Adam away from God. Eve and Adam found the hanging fruit attractive. So at the suggestion of the adversary of God, they ate, and their eyes were opened to the difference between good and evil. Then they were removed from the garden, and the serpent was punished as well. But the serpent accomplished his goal. Personal desire ruled over the reason of God.

Remember this important statement from Peter in the New Testament: "Be sober-minded; watch. Your adversary the devil prowls about as a roaring lion seeking someone to devour" (1 Pet. 5.8). This has not changed. Once we were removed from the perfection of God's presence, sin was all around us. By virtue of being outside of the perfection of God there was sin. But Jesus changed this (see Eph. 2).

Jesus, who was a man just as I am and a person as we all are, though tempted in every way such as we are, was without sin (see Heb. 4:15). Because Jesus was the Sacrificial Lamb of God we have the way of salvation through His death on the cross, as He became our eternal sacrifice. God was pleased to bruise our Lord even though Jesus was innocent (see Isa. 53:10). The pleasure God found in sacrificing Jesus on the cross was derived from the ability of His creation to have the ability to reconcile themselves by being obedient to our Lord and Christ. Jesus was made to be sin on our behalf that when we do as our Lord has commanded, we would be reconciled to God (see 2 Cor. 5). Because of Jesus's sacrifice, we may be partakers in His divine nature, to escape the corruption of the world through lust (see 2 Pet. 1:4). We have been made alive to God because of Jesus! (see Eph. 2). The Bible is clear about this! Read again what the effect of our baptism dose as Paul explained this to the Romans (see Rom. 6). I cannot say it enough what Paul taught is no different than what Jesus told Nicodemus that "unless one is born of water and the Spirit, he cannot enter the kingdom of God." This was to lay the foundation of the way of our salvation. This is how we all get back to God. Your personal belief structure does not change this! Jesus Christ's death and our willingness to be partakers of His death through baptism is essential for our dying to sin; for the removal of our sin. Our living according to the Spirit of God is essential for reconciling our thoughts to how God desires us to live. We cannot desire the things that separate us from God if we expect to be with God. If we believe we can have salvation another way than what Jesus gave and His apostles have taught, this is wrong. That would put us back in sin! There is no private interpretation of Scripture! God has given it!

"And so we have the prophetic word confirmed, which you do well to heed as a light that shines in a dark place, until the day dawns and the morning star rises in your hearts; knowing this first, that no prophecy of Scripture is of any private interpretation, for prophecy never came by the will of man, but holy men of God spoke as they were moved by the Holy Spirit." (2 Pet. 1:19-21).

Thank God for His mercy and grace, for by these we have salvation! From the beginning, we have received favor as the created of God and for the last 2,000 years we can be united to Him through our Lord and Savior Jesus Christ!

But our error continues almost unabated. Man mostly refuses to submit to God! We are in a time much like before. Most people do not want to hear or endure the doctrine of God but instead would rather listen to men who teach according to their desires. This really has never changed. "But according to their own desires, because they have itching ears, they will heap up for themselves teachers and they will turn their ears away from the truth, and be turned to fables" (2 Tim. 4:3–4).

We are transitioning here. Though the adversary is always looking to cause confusion, we have the truth of God still with us. But this truth is taken away from us by the sheer number of people on this earth who adhere to what they believe is right based on their own thoughts and desires. Remember, it is our selfish desire that separated us from God.

Just look at our current political climate. The killing of babies is considered a right. Men and boys dressing as girls is also a right. These lost people are even able to compete as girls in athletics. Girls are likewise dressing as boys. Something is not right here.

This is why democracy fails a society. The mob believes or desires a certain way, and they complain and reason according to their lusts that they are right. People become complacent and the law is of no effect. As a result, you get what happened in Germany during the first half of the twentieth century: the National Socialist Party ruled and the world fell apart. Look at Cuba and Venezuela now. It is the same thing. Socialism kills. When people crave power at almost any cost wrong is bound to occur. We all know this to be true because Jesus was led as a lamb to the slaughter by those He came to save! Why? Mob rule. The law was made of no effect!

When the mob tells you something is true, that thing is likely to be false. Certainly we do not live in a perfect world. So, you essentially have three choices: run, run fast, or stand your ground, girded with the truth of God. Just recently we have seen what the mob desires and it was not reason. When you seek to justify your manner of life in the same way as what you are protesting, you are wrong. Jesus said "If Satan casts out Satan, he is divided against himself. How then will his kingdom stand?" (Matt. 12:26). It will not!

In the beginning was the Word, and the Word was the truth of God. Two thousand years ago, that Word brought forth the teachings we need to understand to be right with God. To be right with God, we need to do as God has said. God has instructed us from the beginning of time and it is time we listen to God instead of popular teachers, who have other motives behind their teachings. Salvation without baptism is a good example of their error.

Use your reason here. I have already proved this to be true using words from our Lord. Baptism is necessary for salvation because baptism is how you die to sin and walk in newness of life with our God. This should be simple to understand, but it isn't. People think you can live in sin and be right with God! Wrong. Modern-day denominational teachers—and I include Catholics here—make baptism what they desire it to be. Scripture is quite clear concerning what baptism is and what it does. As much as the masses would like to change what is written, it is not going to change what God has given to us.

I want to talk a little more about baptism and our salvation. In the denominational arena, there are many who erroneously say that the word "for" in Acts 2:38 is actually "because." This claim supports their erroneous teachings. Word usage does not support this denominational reasoning, and it is therefore false.

The actual Greek word is *eis*, which simply denotes "an entrance into."[8] We can look at every instance in the Bible where *eis* is used

---

[8] "Eis." Blue Letter Bible. Accessed May 19, 2020. https://www. blueletterbible.org/lang/lexicon/lexicon.cfm?Strongs=G1519&t=NKJV

and come to the logical conclusion that what denominationalists say is false. But what if we come to this logical conclusion and you are still unable to grasp this contextual understanding—what then?

Consider: Did Peter say, "Repent and be baptized because your sins have been forgiven"? No. Peter told us to repent and be baptized for the forgiveness of sins. Why would Peter tell the Jews gathered on the day of Pentecost that their sins were already forgiven when those people asked, "Men and brethren what shall we do?" (see Acts 2:37). If those gathered on the day of Pentecost were already forgiven of their sins, why would they ask what they needed to do and why would they then need to repent and be baptized and live to the Spirit of God? Isn't this repentance? This does not make sense. It especially does not make sense in light of John 3:5, in which Jesus said we need to born of water and the Spirit to enter the Kingdom of God.

If we were saved before our sins were removed and before we learned we needed to live to God, then God would be an unjust God, and the people who died in the Old Testament were unjustly forced to live lives that God never intended all people to live. This is what Billy Graham and Franklin Graham would have you to believe! (There are others who teach this error also, so be wise.) But God is not unjust. Applying simple reason to Scripture verifies this. Was Jesus joking when He said, "If you love Me, obey My commandments" (John 14:15)? Think twice before you answer.

Denominational teachers misrepresent the truth of God for their convenience, and this is how it has been for hundreds of years. Billy Graham, Joel Osteen, and many others have misled millions of people away from the truth of the gospel, and others are following. Mob rule is not the way to live as a Christian. To be in Christ, you must follow the Word of Christ.

"I am the vine, you are the branches. He who abides in Me, and I in him, bears much fruit; for without Me you can do nothing. If anyone does not abide in Me, he is cast out as a branch and is withered; and they gather them and throw them into the fire, and they are burned. If you abide in Me, and My words abide in you, you will ask what you desire, and it shall be done for you. By this My Father is glorified, that you bear much fruit; so you will be My disciples." (John 15:5–8)

If our sins were forgiven before our repentance and our baptism, why would Adam and Eve have been removed from the garden of Eden? If we were saved before we did anything worthy of salvation, that would be to say God is unjust. That position is not supported in Scripture. How could we live in the Paradise of God while being in sin? Adam and Eve couldn't do it. God could not have Adam and Eve before Him in sin, and certainly God does not change. So we cannot be in the presence of God without our sins having been washed away. "For I am the LORD, I do not change; therefore you are not consumed, O sons of Jacob" (Mal. 3:6).

Why would God condemn Israel if He imputes salvation to all after Jesus's death? Did God just give up and change? This is what reason would tell us if we believed denominational teachings.

Yes, Jesus's blood now saves us. Hebrews 9 tells us how. In the context of what God desires from us, we must be without sin. The only way to rid ourselves of sin is to be baptized for the remission of sin. The rendering of Romans 6 and 1 Peter 3:21 does not support the idea that we are saved before we are baptized. Rendering *eis* into "because of" is entirely wrong and deceitful. It is the doctrine of demons and therefore wrong.

To demonstrate, look at Matthew 8:28: "When He had come to [*eis*] the other side, into [*eis*] the country of the Gergesenes, there met Him two demon possessed men, coming out of the tombs."

If we use the reasoning of those caught up in denominationalism (mob rule based on what "I believe in my heart"), then we would render Matthew 8:28 as "When He had come [because] the other side, [because] the country of the Gergesenes, there met Him two demon possessed men, coming out of the tombs."

This does not make any sense. For it to make sense, we would need to rewrite the Bible to conform to this error. But this has not been done. We cannot change what God has specifically given us to follow.

Correctly, we are to repent and be baptized for the remission of our sins. Otherwise, if our sins are already forgiven, why would we need to repent? And why would Jesus "because the other side?"

Correct rendering of God's Word is imperative for us to know the truth of God's Word. We become partakers of God's grace when we do what God has commanded, not according to our own private interpretations. The Bible says what it means. Do not be deceived!

But millions of people have been and still are being deceived; especially the young. Millions have not done as Paul tells Timothy in 2 Timothy 2:15. They have not studied. Millions, perhaps billions of people have not studied. They have only thought in their hearts that what was said to them by Billy Graham was the truth of God. It was not! What Billy Graham and the other denominational teachers have given their listeners were only half-truths. Based on what they teach or have taught in the past, they do and did not believe what Jesus said to Nicodemus in John 3:5, what He said to the apostles in Matthew 28:18–20, what Paul tells the Romans in Romans 6, and what Peter says in 1 Peter 3:21: "There is also an antitype which now saves us—baptism (not the removal of the filth of the flesh, but the answer of a good conscience toward God), through the resurrection of Jesus Christ." Certainly if we do not believe our faith in God is built by understanding God we will never be able to comprehend how to build our faith in God (see Rom. 10:17).

These denominational teachers are knowledgeable men, but they believe the lie that you do not need to be baptized to be saved. This is in direct contradiction of Jesus's final words as recorded in Matthew 28. Is repentance not needed to be at one with God? Do we keep on sinning that the grace of God keeps on abounding more and more? (see Rom. 6:1). Is it true we do not need to do as Jesus Himself has said, to be born of water and the Spirit? Are you sure?

When we give our lives over to living as God desires, we renew our minds as Paul instructed in Romans 10:17 and 12:2, Peter said in 2 Peter 1:5–11 and Jesus said in the gospels. When we renew our minds to God, we fulfill what God said about being baptized for the remission of our sins. We therefore have been born of water and the Spirit. We are to die to sin by being baptized for the remission of our sin (see Rom. 6:4). We are to live our lives unto God. We have been given the commandment not to let sin reign in our mortal bodies any longer that we should obey its lust! (see Rom. 6:12).

What we all need to understand is that what Jesus, Peter, Luke, Paul, and the other writers of the New Testament have given to us is the truth of God. Scripture reasons this to be true. The rendering of what is known as Strong's number G1519, *eis*, does not mean "because," and there are 1,513 verses in the New Testament that prove what I say is true.

But even if for some reason we can render *eis* as "because," should we believe what men have said is correct almost two thousand years later over what God Himself actually gave to us? Your sins are not washed away because Jesus died on the cross unless you are baptized for the remission of you sins, "because" unless you have died to sin, you will not be raised in newness of life.

Being baptized "because" your sins have been forgiven is a false teaching and contradicts Romans 6. When you study God's

Word, God's Word and common sense will tell you this—unless, of course, you think the mob is right.

No Bible I have ever seen has the rendering of "because" your sins have been forgiven. Commentaries describe this as the case and many other things are said concerning what baptism is for, but this is not from God. These commentaries were written by men and women with agendas, kind of like the Democratic and Republican parties. If 1 Peter 3:21 tells us we are saved through baptism, and if we become dead to sin when we are baptized as in Romans 6, doesn't it make sense that we need to be baptized for our sin to be removed? Until our sins are removed, we cannot be in the presence of the Almighty. You must remember that Jesus has all authority, and as Jesus told Nicodemus, we must be born of "water and the Spirit" or we will not enter the kingdom of God. This mortifying of the body of sin to God and renewal of our minds to God are essential if we are again to be with God.

So I will ask again: Am I now to listen to men and women with specific doctrinal agendas who were not with Jesus when He walked upon the earth and gave the commandments? If we were to do this, we would be denying God. What we really need to ask ourselves is this: Should we obey God or men? Look to Acts 5:29 for your answer and to the men who received direct revelation from God. Denominationalism is from men, not God. Baptism is necessary for your salvation because Jesus has said it is.

Remember, if we reason by way of our desires, we are not reconciling ourselves to God. For us to live correctly as God has made known to us, we must reconcile ourselves to God. Not ourselves.

15

Our Separation and Our Uniting

THINK ABOUT THIS. When Adam and Eve sinned, they were separated from God. This is how we remain if we are not reconciled to God. God has told us how to be reconciled (see John 3:5, 2 Cor. 5:20). As I hope you know by now, the Bible gives us all we need to know how to be reconciled to God.

Once you read, your eyes will be opened to God, and you should know the way we are to live our lives is within the context of God. We know therefore our reconciliation is through baptism because of what our Lord has said and living as God would have you live ensures this.

If you listen to modern-day denominational preachers, the sin of Adam and Eve is of no consequence. On the face of things, it seems popular teachers do not understand we need to come back to God as He has said. They may even tell you that you can just go on your way, believing in but not obeying God and that God sent Jesus so that everyone could be saved, no matter what they believe. According to the doctrine of demons, denominational Christians will tell you to say a "sinners prayer" and all will be well. Neither our God nor Jesus gave any indication that such a prayer needed to be said in order to be saved, but still, the denominationalists profess that when you say this prayer, you will be saved. This is not substantiated by Scripture anywhere. In fact, this denominational reasoning nullifies all that God says to be true. This is just how the adversary likes it: desire over reason and the renewal of our minds to God.

Application: How many times have you gone to a funeral where the deceased is now automatically going to Paradise to be with God? More often than not, this is the case. Knowing what you know now after reading what I have written you should know this is not true. If someone in their life has not done as Jesus said they, you, me are not going to be with God in the end.

As I have said already since Adam and Eve ate from the Tree of the Knowledge of Good and Evil, we have been separated from God. They ate because of their lack of belief in God. Why wouldn't we be saved if we believed and did what God has said will save us? The act of disobedience separated us from God, and obeying will reconcile us back to Him. Was not this the purpose of our Lord? (see Rom. 5.) When we collectively began to live according to our own thoughts, away from what God authorized for us, we walk away from God. We succumb to the error of what we think, which has nothing to do with God. Adam and Eve's thoughts were changed away from what God had given them and this is how it is today, only magnified.

Remember, Jesus has told us we need to be dead to sin and alive in the Spirit if we want to be in the Kingdom of God. We have instructions on how we can become dead to sin. Yet so-called God-fearing men and women teach that baptism is not necessary. What are they doing? These who teach this doctrine are teaching the doctrine of demons, just as Paul told Timothy (see 1 Tim. 4:1–2). These people are intentionally misleading the souls of millions of people, who rely on the masses instead of on the eternal Word of God. Those who teach baptism is not necessary for our salvation do not understand the relationship we are to have with our God. These people are very dangerous, and we should have nothing to do with them (see 2 Cor. 6:17, 7:1). Again, mob rule has proven to be wrong.

The Word of God is clear in its explanation of how we are to be united with God. God sent His Son to be a sacrifice for our sin. When we are "born of water and the Spirit," we can have life with God again, through our Lord and Savior, Jesus Christ.

Jesus said, "If you love Me, obey My commandments" (John 14:15). We need to make a decision to obey our Lord, who told the apostles to baptize for the remission of sins. In Acts 2:38, you see the apostles doing this very thing. Should we then not believe that when we are baptized, we die to sin so that we can be raised in newness of life? The evidence is right before us. But many allow themselves to be deceived simply because they do not "study to show themselves approved" (2 Tim. 2:15). They instead trust preachers who line their pockets with the money of their followers. Jesus did not line His pockets with anyone's money, did He?

When you study God's Word, you will see that in the book of Acts, not one person was right with God who was not baptized for the remission of their sins. God's Word is clear. Do not jump to conclusions. I have died to sin through baptism, to be raised in newness of life at the returning of our Lord and our God. I am renewed in the spirit of my mind. I live for God. This is why being dead to sin through baptism is necessary. Everyone sins and everyone needs salvation to be right with God. Since the garden of Eden, this has been true. The only one who can change the terms of our entrance into Paradise is God Himself. There is not one theologian alive today who can change these terms!

Consider our Lord and the thief at their crucifixion. Jesus told the thief he would be in Paradise. Jesus did not say this to anyone else. Jesus made the terms of salvation for this person. Jesus has this authority. We do not have this authority. Salvation is not ours to give, especially as sinners. We have not sacrificed our lives for anyone. If you are honest, you will understand what I am saying. Think about this! Men and women have no right to change what God alone has given.

Knowing this, my search for purpose is over. My obedience to God has made my separation from God into my unification with God. This is because I know God and what He has given to us. I know where the Higher Power is, and it is God. So please hear my message as I tell you of our need to put our God first in all that we do. God wants us to come back to Him according to what has been written for our learning (see Jude 3). You need to know this.

Our uniting with God depends upon our obedience to God, regardless of what people tell you. If what people tell you does not coincide with what God has prepared in the Word of God, then it is not true. Do not believe them. The Word of God is clear (see 2 Jo. 1:8 – 10).

16

Searching for God and the Cultural Revolution

THE WAY WE live our lives according to the cultures we create does not endear us to God. God has made Himself known to us. If we want to be right with God, we will build our cultures around what God has given.

In the beginning, God created us. God gave us the way we are to live our lives. The understanding we need to have about God is not a matter of who we believe we are or what we do. You could be an innocent person who does not bother anyone, the most conniving politician in the world, or the most "woke" social media guru on the planet. You could be some homosexual priest preaching an "enlightened" gospel to gather people to you. You could also be some rapper who all of the sudden finds God and devotes himself to God. But nothing you do of your own volition is going to make God into who you desire Him to be. This type of living is without the understanding of God and how most of us live our lives. If we were truly woke as it is said, we would understand this simple truth. More people would be teaching that our reuniting to God, our salvation comes through our Lord. The example that Israel left us should be enough to confirm that we cannot make God into what we desire and live correctly. For example, I am not justified to God based on my own reasoning through the lens of my culture. I need to look to the Word of God to find my justification from God and the Bible is that way.

"For whatever things were written before were written for our learning, that we through the patience and comfort of the Scriptures might have hope" (Rom. 15:4). God is and has always been who He is. He does not exist according to our own desires. Man's decree of something does not nullify what God has said and done. You need to understand this about God.

There is a mountain of evidence before us that tells us who our Lord is, where He came from, and from where He reigns. God's Son was pronounced King of the Jews before His crucifixion by those He came to save (see Matt. 27:37). God Himself said "This is My beloved Son. Hear Him!" (Luke 9:35). But we (Israel) killed our Lord and our God for the pronouncement that our cultures and personal practices are more important than what our Lord came to do. Israel is our example to this purpose. Our Lord and Savior came to seek and save that which was lost (see Matt. 18:11). This is Israel and this is us. Looking at us today and Israel yesterday, most of us do not care. Instead, the mob covets each day as if the day itself were the god we are to serve. Examples that exist from before are largely ignored as we progress into a future of that which we covet.

The main evidence we have to tell us that the existence of our God is true and what we will be if we do not change our way of living is the existence of the nation of Israel. The history of Israel's beginning and ending as God's people is contained within the pages of our Bible. But even with the nation of Israel in our midst and the fact Israel was the chosen people at one time, we have yet to realize that the people Jesus came to save first are the ones who killed Him (see Rom. 1:16). Very little has changed. The message of salvation continues to fall on deaf ears. Israel is not the chosen nation of God any longer. Instead, the chosen nation of God are those who "volunteer in the day of Your power" (Ps. 110:3). We are those who are "born of water and the Spirit."

Many people searching for a higher power will never come to knowledge of the truth. Many are searching for "something" that will prove to them the existence of God, but they never look to what God has actually given to us so that we may know Him. They have no faith in God. They only trust in what they see. They are unable to use their ability to reason the way of God though this way is written into everything about us. In addition, we are constantly bombarded by false teachings about who our God is and other man-made doctrines, gods and creeds.

People are always looking for a sense of purpose according to how they believe their lives should be. In this search, which is not new, people have looked away from God. They have challenged His authority because they do not believe in what God has given to us. Perhaps they do not even know about God. What began with the simple deception of the adversary in the garden has separated us from God. We have grown to believe our cultures can dictate the way we think. For some odd reason, we believe we have the ability to make the terms upon which God exists to us. Israel was condemned for serving Baal and Ashtoreth, not God. Israel was condemned for serving God according to their own ways of thinking. In the same way, we will be condemned if we do not turn to God.

Remember the adversary in Genesis 3? By now, how could you forget? Let me tell you, thinking we have the ability to set the terms of our relationship with God is wrong. The truth is, if you want to be with God, you must submit yourself to the will of God based on the terms He has given. For us today, this is easy in comparison to the time of the Exodus.

We have had the written Word of God with us for over thirty-five hundred years. Looking for God becomes a straightforward matter of trusting what has always been written with what has been right there before us. How many people are unable to trust because of some erroneous lifestyle or belief? How many are just not willing to accept the truth of God for this reason? How is anyone going to trust God when they will not even study God's Word? Or they add to it, thinking their culture or self-ascribed religion is what dictates the God of our creation?

As the old saying goes, you can lead a horse to water, but you can't make him drink. The horse is not going to drink unless he is thirsty. There are a lot of dehydrated horses out there in the religious world, filling themselves up with false religion! What people need to do is grow their faith in God. It is written, "Faith comes by hearing, and hearing by the word of God" (Rom. 10:17).

We cannot grow our faith in God if we refuse to believe that the Bible contains God's Word, and that we cannot change it. God does not change, as the prophet Malachi tells us (see Mal. 3:6). But we do change, and how we change does not dictate who God is. We do not make God.

Today, there are many people who acknowledge God exists. But when they try to come to grips with their desire to serve God in some way, they only look to what they are able to comprehend or what makes them feel good. They end up becoming followers of what they "feel" is right, what they have been born into, or what famous men or women tell them; convenience and the pop culture rules in their lives.

The apostle Paul tells us to do much differently. Paul says to "put on the new man" (Eph. 4:24). Perhaps people live in their own way because this is the easy thing to do? We justify our beliefs about God by our ancestry or cultural associations. Paramount in our ability to find God is using our understanding to trust what God has given to us. We build our faith through our understanding of the story God has provided. The truth of God is and has always been before us. Most just do not believe it to be true.

We have denied what God has given to us because we are what we call "individual moral agents" of our own making.

Instead we should be submitting ourselves to God. We allow what our culture has become to erode our ability to understand what God has done for us. We justify our false beliefs by saying that our lives and the culture we live in can dictate who God is. Again, this is false. We are all one people in the eyes of our God. There are no differences between us except the cultures we create, which have proven to be very destructive to living according to what God has given. Don't all lives matter? Why isolate one group over another? We are all people who live in sin. We cannot expect perfection of someone else when we ourselves are not perfect. We can be perfect when we are born of water and the Spirit as God has given. We should be different, but yet we are sinners. This is why Christ died. We who have died to Christ and put Him on still must live amongst the error of those who live according to their own dictates (see Rom. 6). Didn't Jesus do the same?

There are many avenues people have gone down over the centuries, all leading to error. There is only one God and one way of getting to God. God Himself has given us this way, and we can know it. Who alive has not heard of Jesus Christ, the Messiah? If Jesus were not real, the name of our Lord would have vanished long ago just as Gamaliel spoke (see Acts 5:33-42). It hasn't done so. Our God is known, and it is safe to say that those who hold to their cultural beliefs over what our God has given to us are indeed in error.

How did we get to the point of questioning who God is and constantly adding our own thoughts and ways to what He has given to us? This is really the ultimate question we are dealing with. Genesis 3 explains our lack of reasoning in detail. We should not overlook the effects of what happened in Genesis 3, where the serpent suggested to Eve that God was a liar. Ever since this time, there has been a steady and constant degradation of human character, leading us away from our God as we create our cultures.

The context of our lives changed when God gave us over to our own ways for not trusting Him. Instead of living within the context God created us for, we now have to place our lives back into the context God gave if we desire to be with God. Today, we do not understand this. Our lack of understanding keeps us from the context we should have with God. We must understand that this was and still is the eternal desire of the adversary. The adversary wants to keep us from our God! Please understand what I am telling you.

When we desire our own ways over what God has given to us, we have walked away from God. This is how mankind is. Your culture does not matter. We do not know this because we do not know God. We suffer from a lack of knowledge of our God and do not even realize that we are constantly battling to come back to Him. As a community—really, a world community—we have not supported each other by God's Word of truth. We have used our lack of knowledge and our cultures to confound people into believing half-truths and lies.

Understand that "there is only one Lord, one faith, and one baptism" (Eph. 4:5). Consider 2 Thessalonians 2:11, and do not believe what is false. Any teaching other than that of our Lord is false, whether it is called Christianity or anything else. You do not need a college degree to understand the salvation of God, nor do you need to be ordained by man to teach the Word of God. Obedience of faith in God and study are all that is needed. If we must build a culture, we need to build on the culture of our Lord and Savior Jesus Christ who died to give us the only way to live to God.

So there is hope! If you can explain why all of what I have said is true according to Scripture, believe it, and continue to live the way God desires you to live, you have nothing to worry about. If you think about it, I will have the greater condemnation if what I tell you is false (see James 3:1). If you obey God's Word, you are on the right track and John 3:5 means something to you.

Most people have locked up their ability to reason the things of God within the context of how they live today. They think their thoughts of God, denominationalism, or even the interfaith message is the key to the way to God. Denominationalism, colleges and universities have really confused the simple message of God. We are to endeavor "to keep the unity of the Spirit in the bond of peace" (Eph. 4:3). This is because there is only "one body and one Spirit, just as you were called in on hope of your calling; one Lord, one faith, one baptism; one God and Father of all, who is above all, and through all, and in you all." (Eph. 4:4-6).

I work for a university hospital system. The message of unity in diversity is constantly espoused there. Diversity is celebrated and worshipped rather than the salvation we have available from our God. The message of God is not taught. The message is about diverse ways of serving God, and this is false. Instead, the university perpetuates immoral lifestyles and godless ways of living. The way of God is not taught and in fact it is ignored.

Rarely will a person pick up the Word of God and see the truth of all that has been. This certainly will not be done in the mainstream universities. The unadulterated understanding we should have of God therefore seems to be incomprehensible to many, though it is not. Life has become our diversity and our differences are celebrated instead of God and the way He has given us to live. We cannot know the way of God through humanistic reasoning. Don't let the adversary deceive you. Realize the adversary is still out there (see 1 Peter 5:8). We must rely on God to know the truth of our lives. All we need to do is trust what is and has been written for our learning and understanding by the Holy men of God (see 2 Peter 1:21). Only then are we able to fully comprehend all of what God has given to us.

I wish I did not need to explain this, but I do. This is why I am writing. Without knowing God, we are lost. Today, just as yesterday, if we do not read the Bible and live the way God has given to us, we will be eternally lost.

The words of James are appropriate here: "Therefore submit yourselves to God. Resist the devil and he will flee from you" (James 4:7). The Devil, Satan, and the adversary are one and the same.

As I hope you can understand by now, God is with us through Jesus Christ our Lord, who was sent for the sole purpose of dying as an offering of sin. When we are born of water and the Spirit, we can have our eternal home with God. To understand who God is, we can read the Bible. In that book, we find a congregation of people who gather in the name of our Lord and Savior, Jesus Christ. It is in the name of Jesus that the church gathers. The term "church" refers to this congregation of people. But when it comes to seeking God, the understanding of what the church is has been filtered through a humanistic, denominative process of thought. Why is this true? Why have we come to this point? As I have said, we lack the ability to see God for who He is and the Son He sacrificed on our behalf. Are we to rely on the teachings of men over those of God? Are we not able to understand who God is?

The church is Christ's. Can I own the church that God created? Can anyone start a church in the name of Jesus Christ, according to their private interpretation and implementation of teachings which are not what God has given, and call it the church of our Lord? Are my desires, my culture, or my belief structure what defines the church of our Lord? *No!*

For us to be united in the same mind is to recognize that God began the church through His Son and our Lord, Jesus Christ. The book of Acts explains this.

Our individual characteristics make us who we are, but we must recognize there is only one way to God if we would like to live with our God in eternity and have more harmony on this earth. Our cultures and humanistic desires do not dictate what God has given. We must understand it is God who rules in the kingdom of men (see Dan. 4). Only when we realize God is in control will we be able to find God. Remember, Jesus is King. Therefore, we must submit all we are to His purpose (see Eph. 3).

In the meantime, God patiently endures our lack of understanding. "The Lord is not slack concerning His promise, as some count slackness, but is longsuffering toward us, not willing that any should perish but that all should come to repentance" (2 Pet. 3:9).

Be reconciled to God first, then your culture.

17

Understanding

IN WRITING TO you I desire to help you understand the truth of our God according to what everyone can know from reading God's Word, and not as we feel or conjure in our own minds. As children of God, you are my neighbors and we have work to do. Our work is to understand who God is and what God has done for us. We are doing no one any favors if we continue to ignore what God has placed right in front of us as we only look to the dictates of men for what God gave to us. We all need to follow our Lord's every commandment if we desire to be with God.

Yet in this we fall short. Everyone does; there is no exception. No one is perfect in themselves. Only our Lord was perfect and you should know why by now. You should also know it is through His blood that we have our forgiveness. Jesus paid the price required by God for us to be redeemed. "Christ redeemed us from the curse of the Law, having become a curse for us—(for it is written, "Cursed is everyone who hangs on a tree") (Gal. 3.13), in order that in Christ Jesus "the blessing of Abraham might come to the Gentiles" (Gal. 3.14a) so that we would "receive the promise of the Spirit through faith" (Gal. 3:14b).

Being with God is what I strive for. I believe (see Mark 1:15) I do understand God. This is why I live my life in obedience to the faith once handed down (see Jude 3). I have repented (see Acts

2:38). I have confessed (see Rom. 10:9-10). I have been baptized. I am constantly renewing the Spirit of my mind (see John 3:5; Rom. 12:2). At least this is what I strive for. We can never forget that when we have been baptized, we have been buried with Christ to die to sin. This is how we are perfected in Christ and able to come near to God (see Heb. 10:11–39). Although we can come near to God, do not be as the pope, confused by thinking you have the same authority Jesus has. You do not. We get our authority from our Lord.

I thank God for the grace He has given to us so that we can come to this understanding. Do not let this understanding flee from you. It is precious. Put the way of God within your being. Flee from the Devil and he will flee from you (see James 4:7). When you live to God, then you understand the purpose of your life, even if it may not make sense to you initially. This is why we study. We are God's people, but this fact we do not know. I hope you can see Him now. I hope you can see your need to renew your mind to God.

Since Adam and Eve fell away from God in the garden, not one person has had a perfect relationship with God except our Lord Jesus, our Messiah. This is why Jesus is our perfect sacrifice for sin. Jesus came into the world to save sinners, me and you, that those who seek justice would recognize our Savior. Jesus went to the cross and took our sins upon Himself so we could come to God. Whoever believes in Him, calls on Him, comes to Him, and is born of water and the Spirit will have everlasting life. This is how we come to God!

Do not be misled by those who say differently. They will take Scripture out of context to justify their own desires and cultural beliefs. They say things that are only half true or are plainly false. God's Word is clear about this: "Brethren, join in following my example, and note those who so walk, as you have us for a pattern. For many walk, of whom I have told you often, and now tell you even weeping, that they are the enemies of the cross of Christ:

whose end is destruction, whose god is their belly, and whose glory is in their shame – who set their mind on earthly things" (Phil. 3:18–19).

Regardless of what anyone tells you, always know that what is recorded in God's Word is the truth of what our God has given to us. We must be born of water and the Spirit to enter the Kingdom of God.

Conclusion

WHAT I HOPE I have done is to get you to think about your life and help you see where you are in the plan of God. I hope you understand how important you are to God. God wants to give us His Kingdom to live within. This requires we come to God on the terms He has given. We cannot live in the Kingdom of God according to man-made decrees listening to the erroneous teachings of men and women who hold to another form of doctrine. Remember, Islam, Buddha, Hinduism, the pope, TBN, Joel Osteen, Billy Graham, John Hagee, Joyce Meyer, and the other denominations (Baptist, Lutheran, 7th Day Adventist, etc.) created by men are not going to teach you what you must know to be saved. There is no continuing revelation from God. Study God's Word to show yourself approved to God (2 Tim. 2.15). The Bible is clear.

God is with us, and we must be with God if we desire to be in the Kingdom of God. The grace of God is unstoppable! Do not blame God for your troubles; you are looking in the wrong place. Bring yourself closer to God! Above all, do not use the Lord's name in vain. That is unprofitable. If you want to know and understand about the first-century church, about the church of Christ read the book of Acts and see how the church of Christ became what it is.

As we go about our day-to-day activities, understanding what God has always had before us is hard. It can be difficult or even impossible for us to fathom because "all have sinned and fallen short of the glory of God" (Rom. 3:23). When you read and think about our reality, and understand what God has given to us, you will see we have a continuing need to understand that the once-chosen people of God are still in existence today. It is from them we have our Lord, who has given the world the ability to come back to God. Jesus offered Himself a sacrifice to God on our behalf and the Jews were the conduit for this to happen.

We need to look extensively at what God has prepared for us. We need to examine what has been written in His Word. We need to understand we are to live according to His purpose. We need to seek His Way. Regardless of what the pope or anyone else says, we must not believe it unless it matches the Word of God. Therefore, we need to study just as Paul instructed Timothy in 2 Timothy 2:15. When we do this act of examination, we become able to place ourselves within the framework of what God has given to us. This is how you build your faith in God. This is learning to trust what has been written for our learning.

So be understanding. We will not ever understand who God is until we understand the story of God. Like Abraham and Moses, like our Lord and His apostles, we need to have faith in God. We need to obey our God. Without faithful obedience to God, we become part of the masses who ignore God—to their peril and the peril of all around them. That is us. This is why we suffer. Thus, we must not allow unfamiliarity with who our God is to dictate the course of our lives. We must grow in our understanding of God. Ignoring God is wrong, but it is what we do. Our life's ambition should be to seek and find the King of our lives (see Matt. 7.7). It is through faithful obedience to Jesus that we finally get back to the Kingdom of God. To do otherwise is missing the mark.

Be understanding and learn. Ask questions. Grow your faith in God. Demonstrate your obedience through love and understanding of all that God has given to us. Renew your mind to

God, as the apostle Paul says: "I beseech you therefore, brethren, by the mercies of God, that you present your bodies a living sacrifice, holy, acceptable to God which is your reasonable service. And do not be conformed to this world, but be transformed by the renewing of your mind, that you may prove what is that good and acceptable and perfect will of God" (Rom. 12:1–2).

God be with us all as we learn and grow our faith and turn to God. Take the time to learn about the greatness of our God and your eternal purpose. Follow the instructions of our Lord as if your life depends on it, because our lives do. Remember, we must be born of water and the Spirit if we have any desire to get back to the kingdom of God.

May God bless us as we look to Him.

About the Author

BILL MITCHELL, A student of the Word of God, has been a Christian for more than twenty-five years. He works in the medical field as a respiratory therapist in the Atlanta area. He earned a Bachelor of Science in Business Administration and Economics and an Associates of Science in Respiratory Therapy. His primary goal in life is helping others to know God. He lives in the Atlanta area of Georgia with his wife and daughter. They are active members of Lawrenceville church of Christ.

9 781973 695868

CPSIA information can be obtained
at www.ICGtesting.com
Printed in the USA
BVHW031056150920
588776BV00016B/43